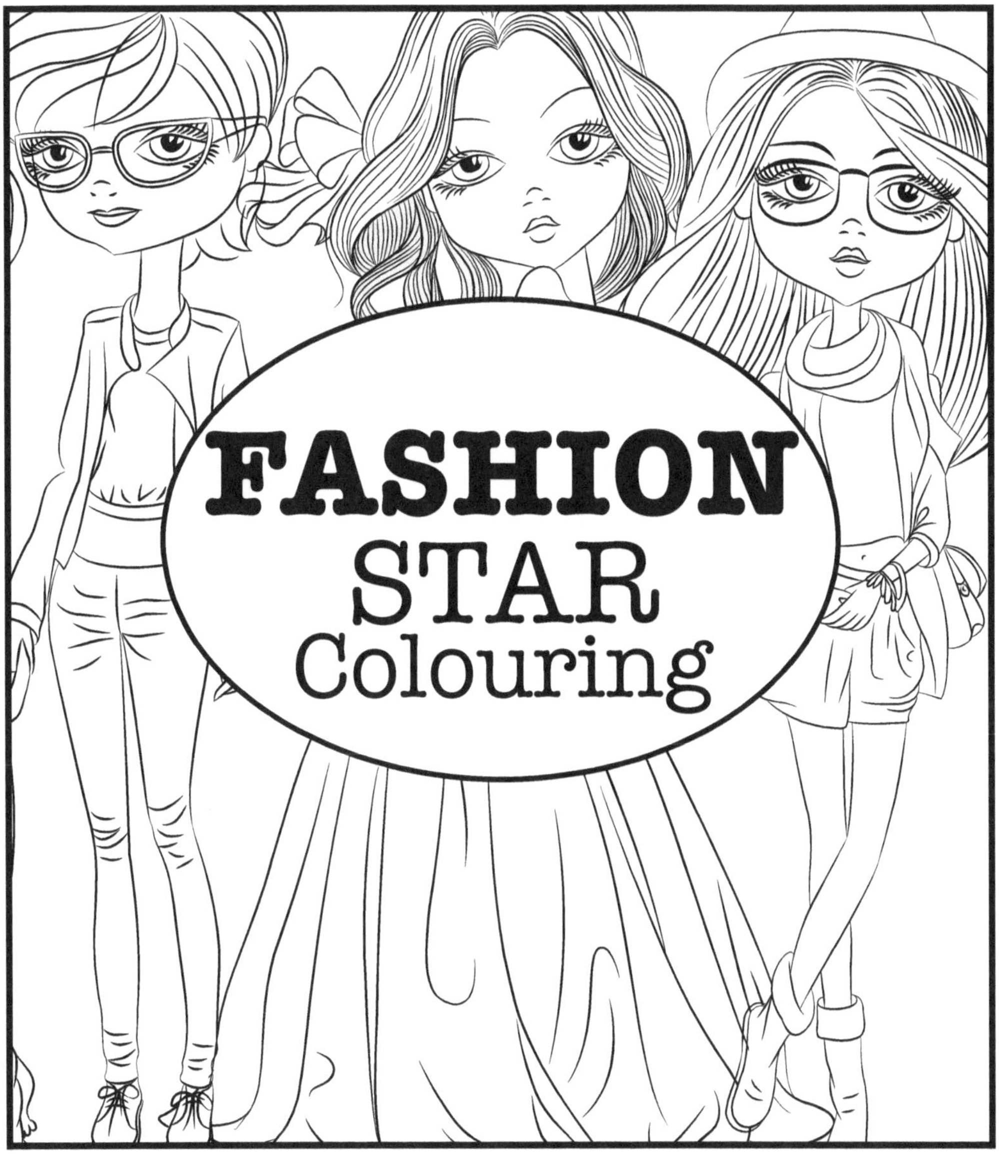

FASHION STAR Colouring

Gorgeous Colouring For Girls **Book 6**

First published in 2016 by Kyle Craig Publishing

Editor: Alison McNicol

Design: Elizabeth James, Julie Anson, Alison McNicol, Shutterstock, Inc.

ISBN: 978-1-78595-123-7

A CIP record for this book is available from the British Library.

A Kyle Craig Publication

www.kyle-craig.com

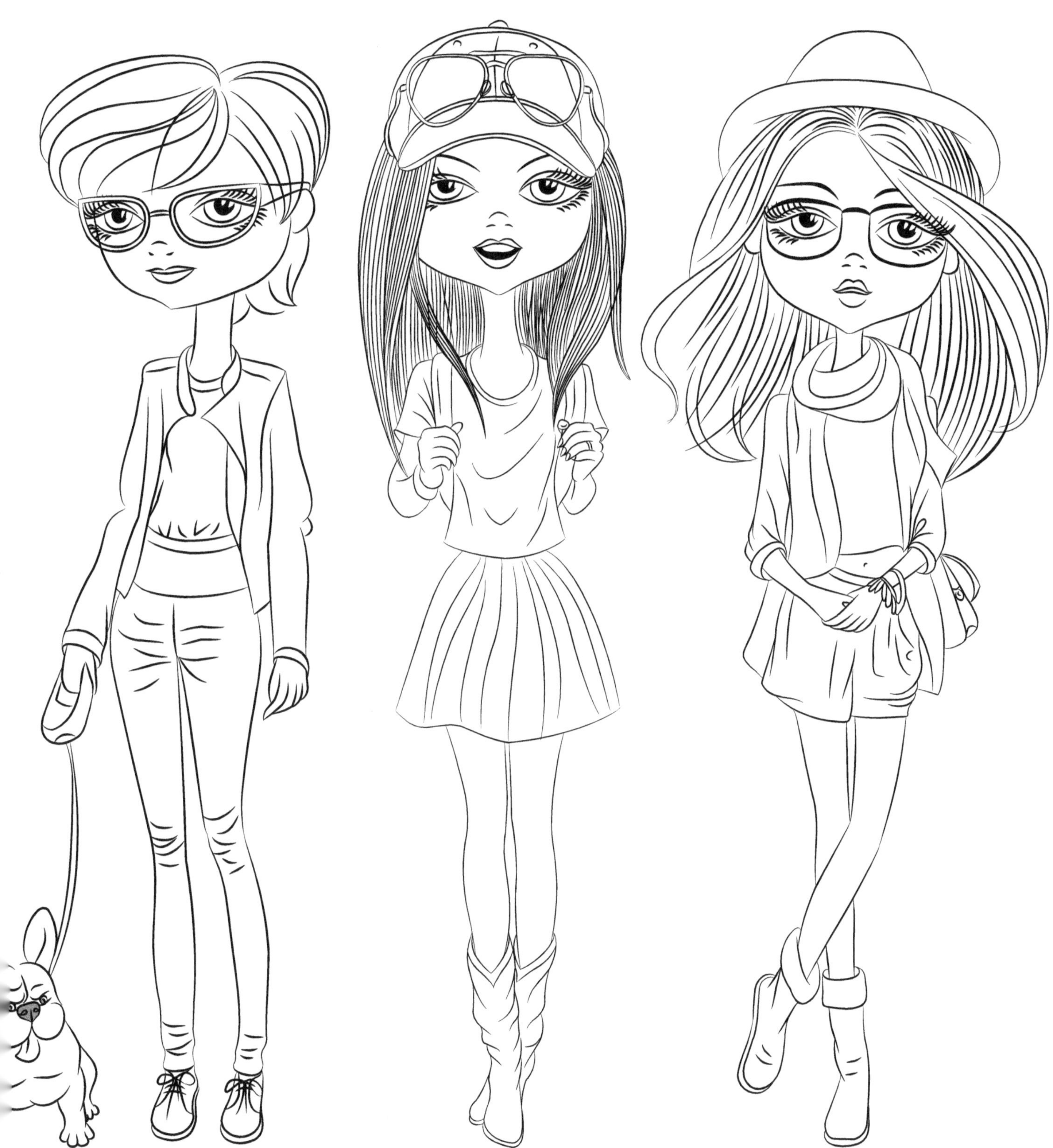

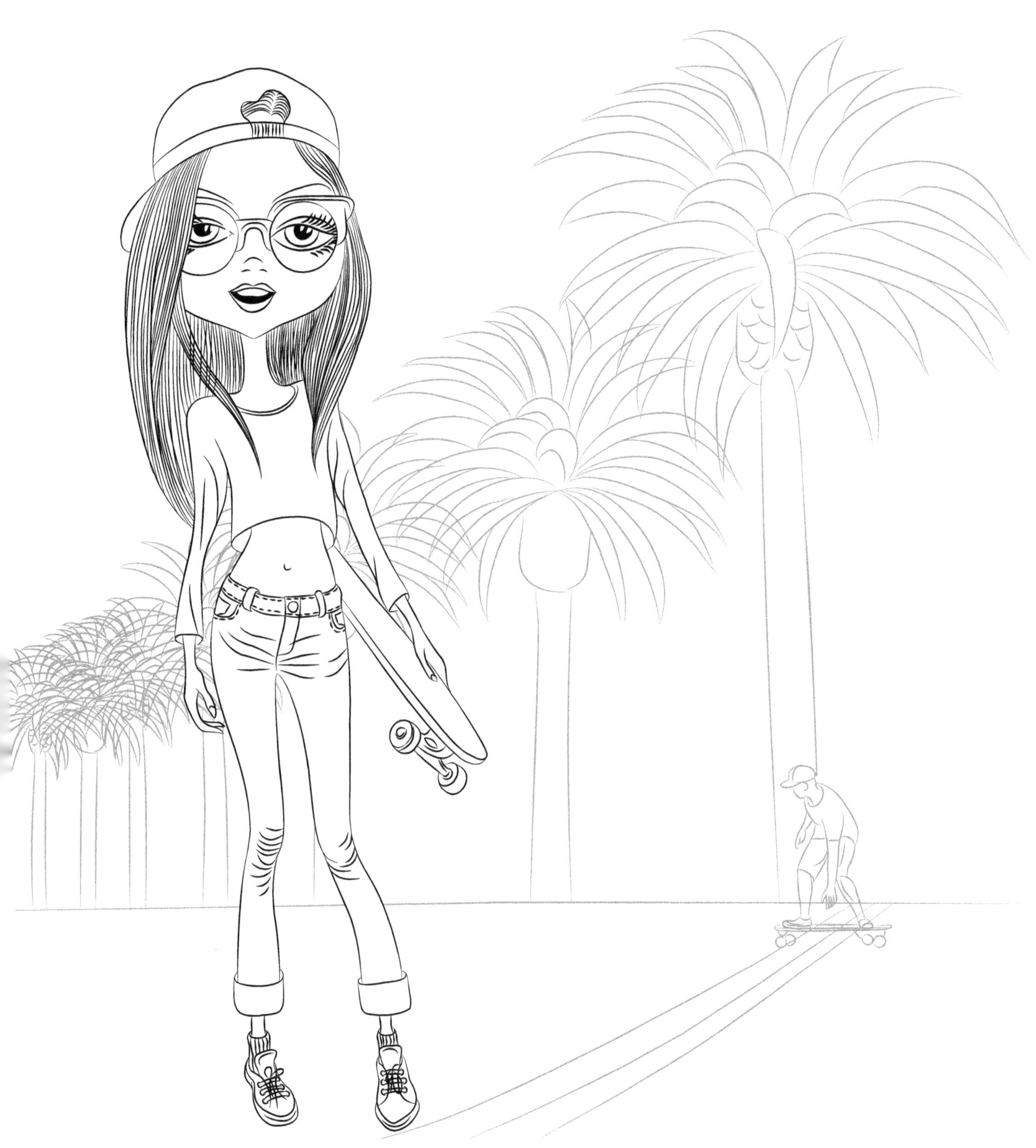

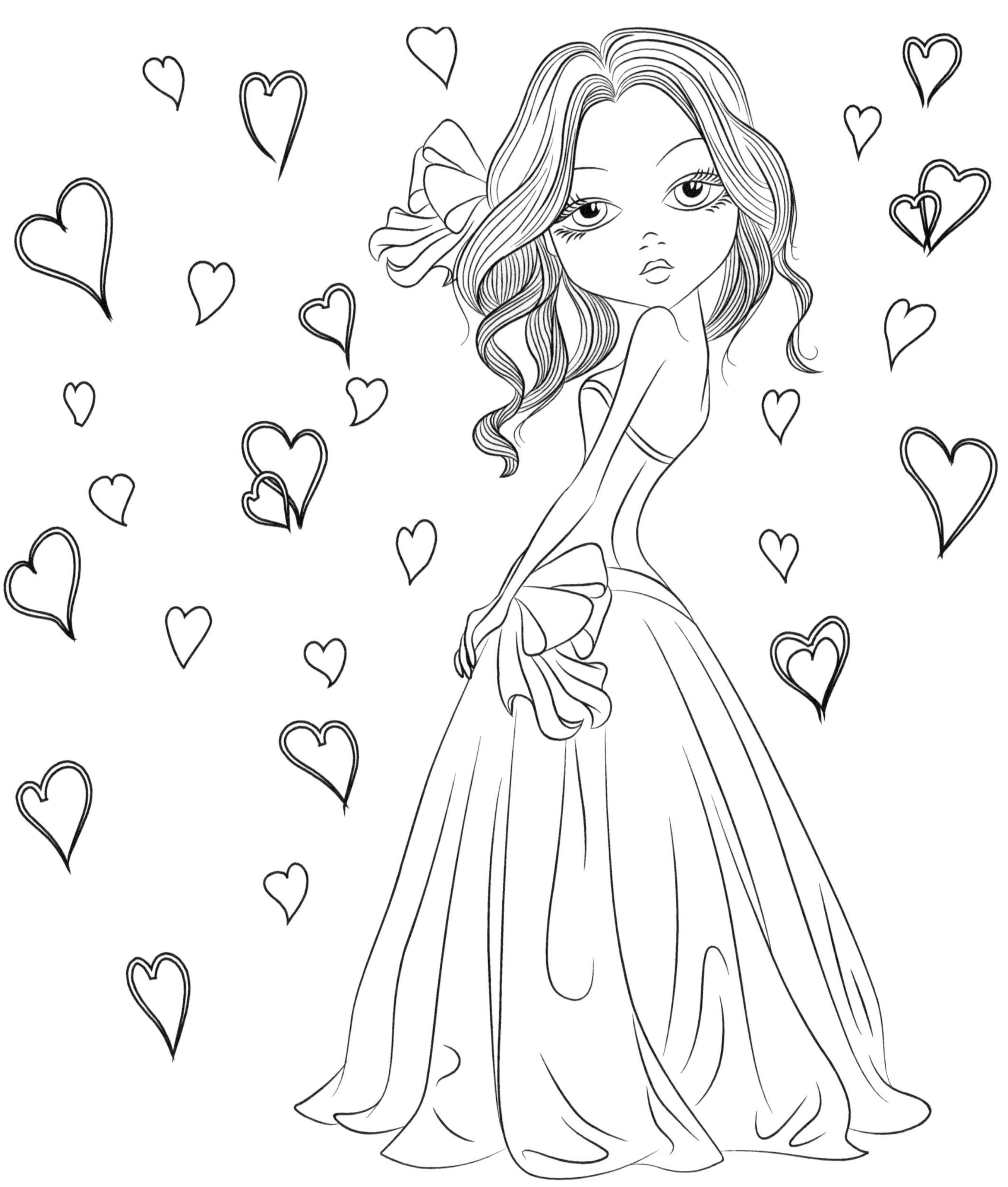

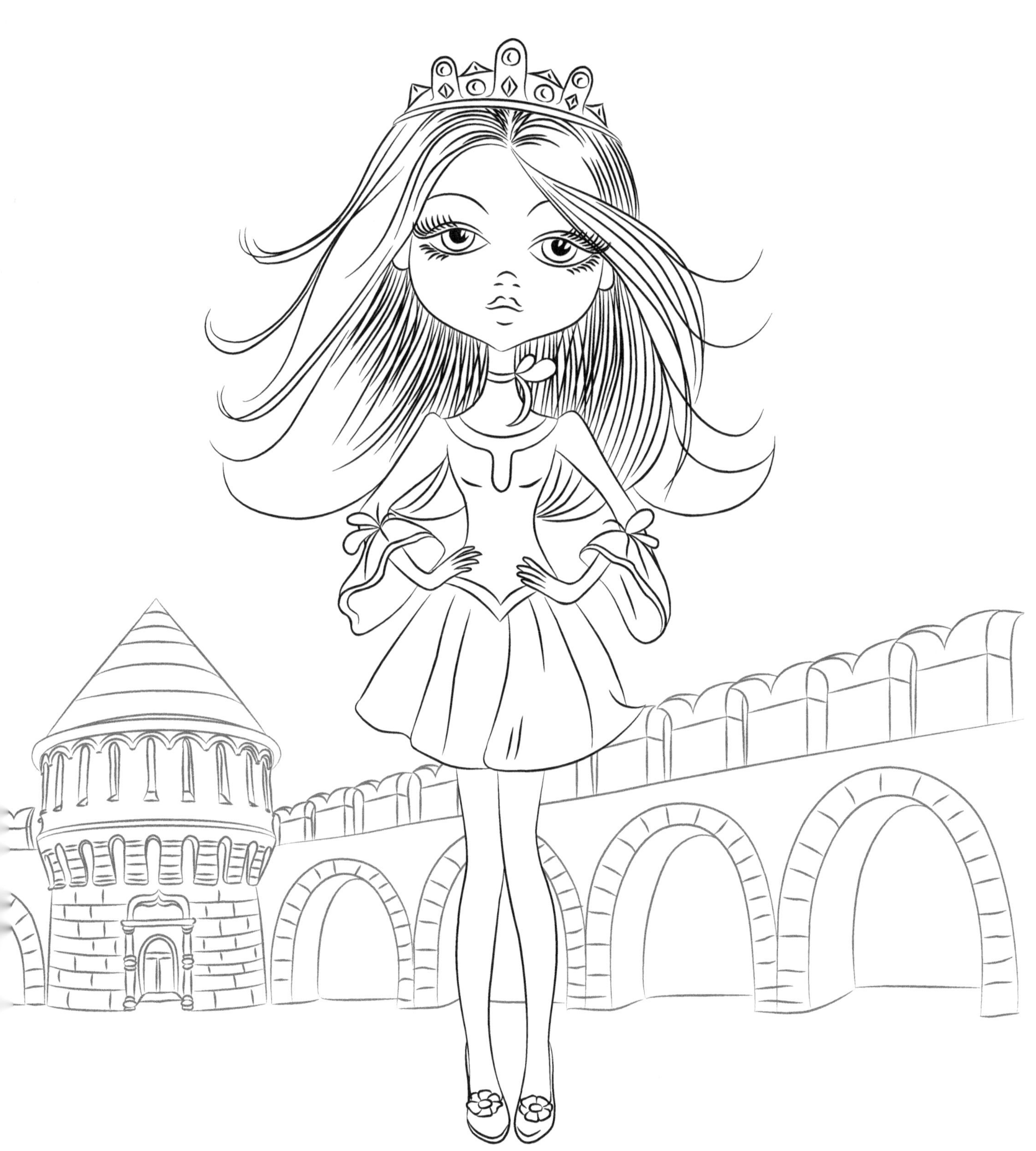

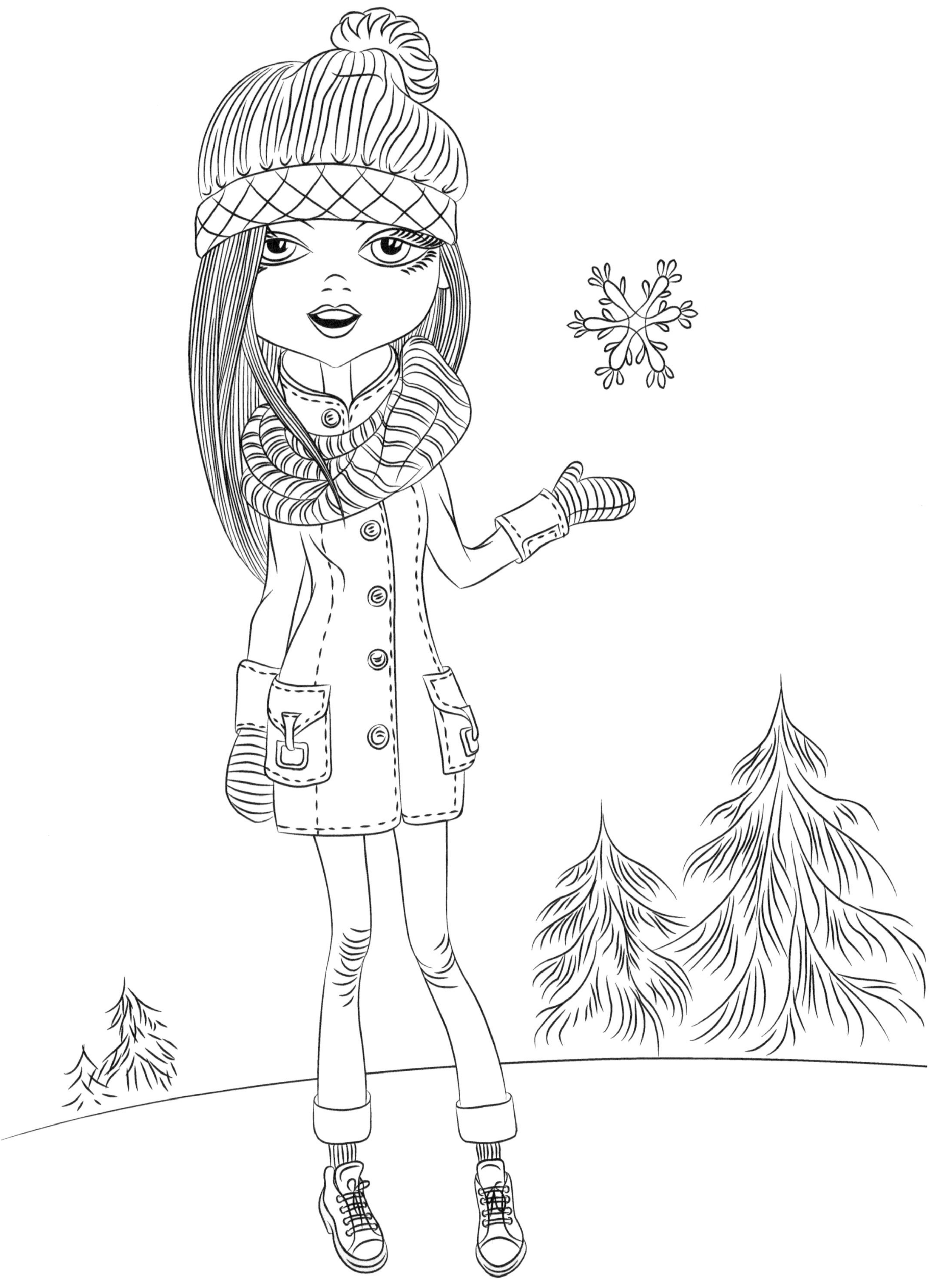

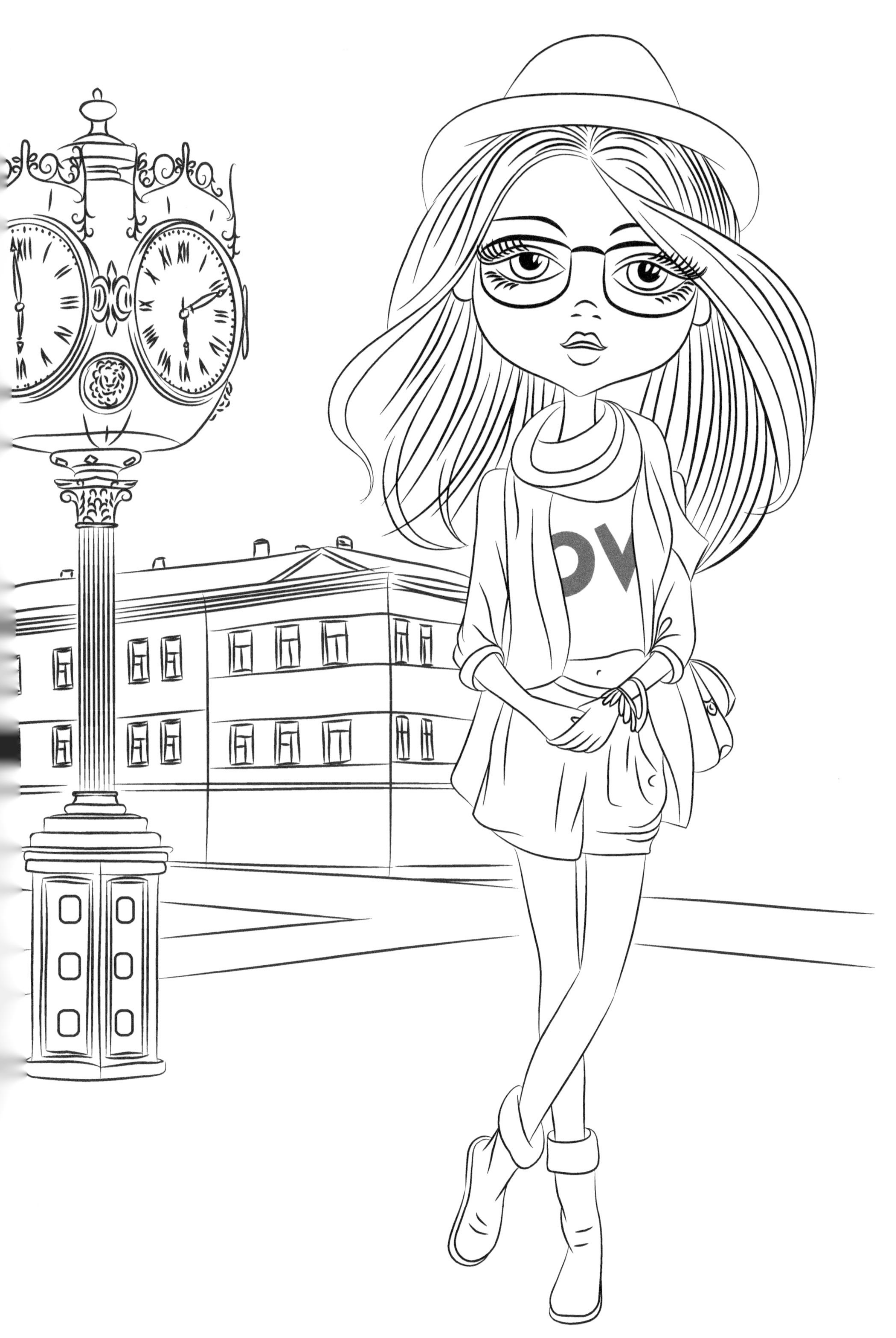
OV

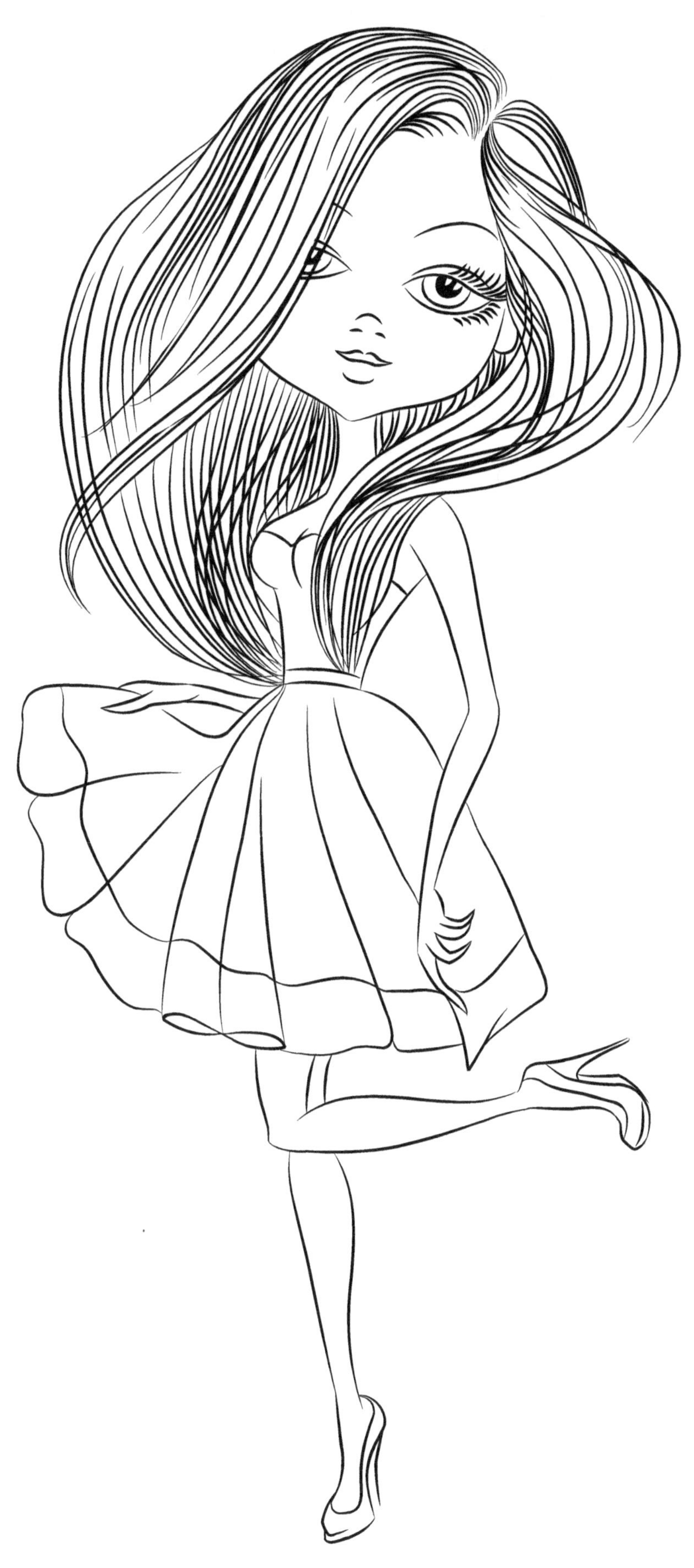

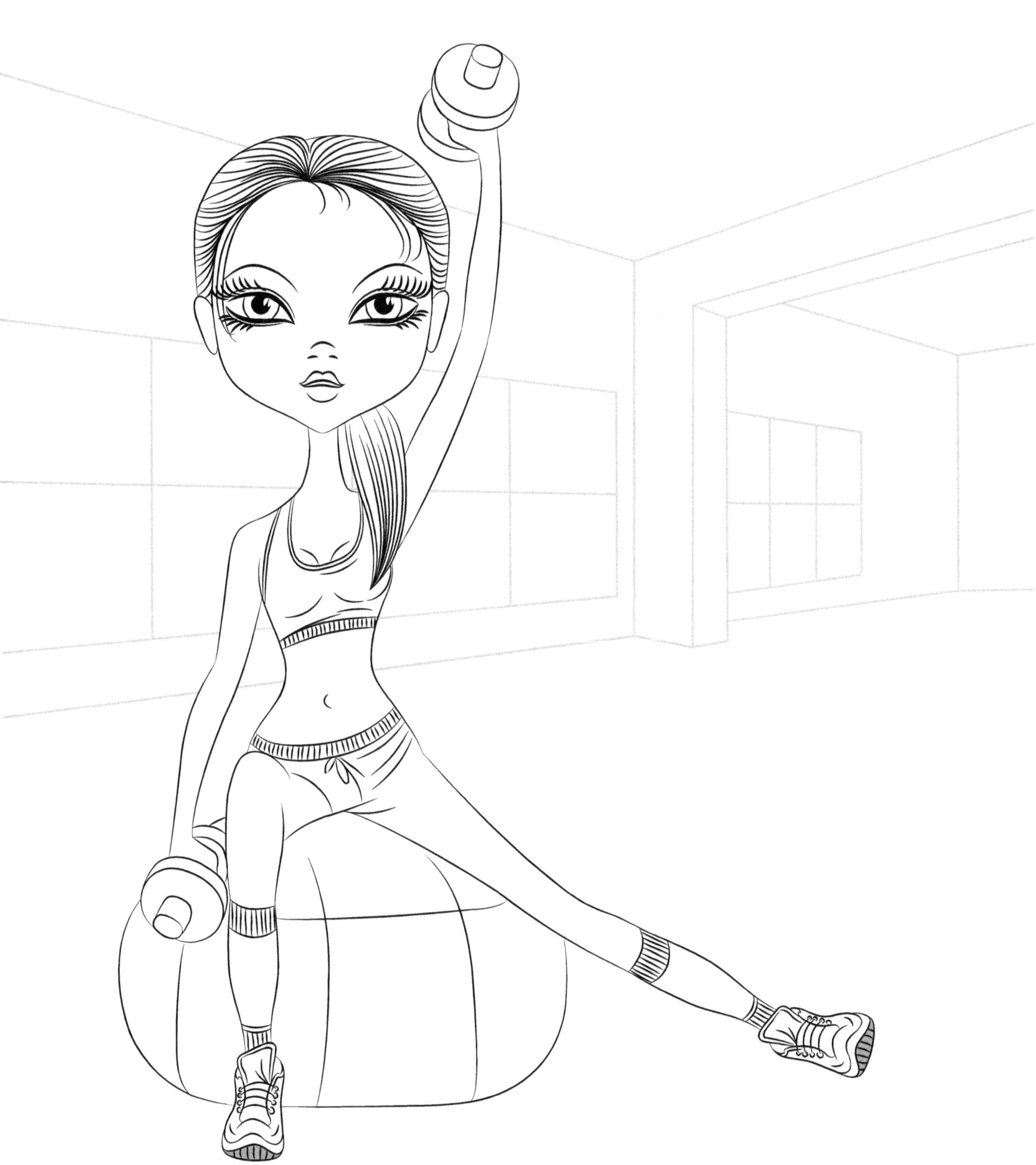

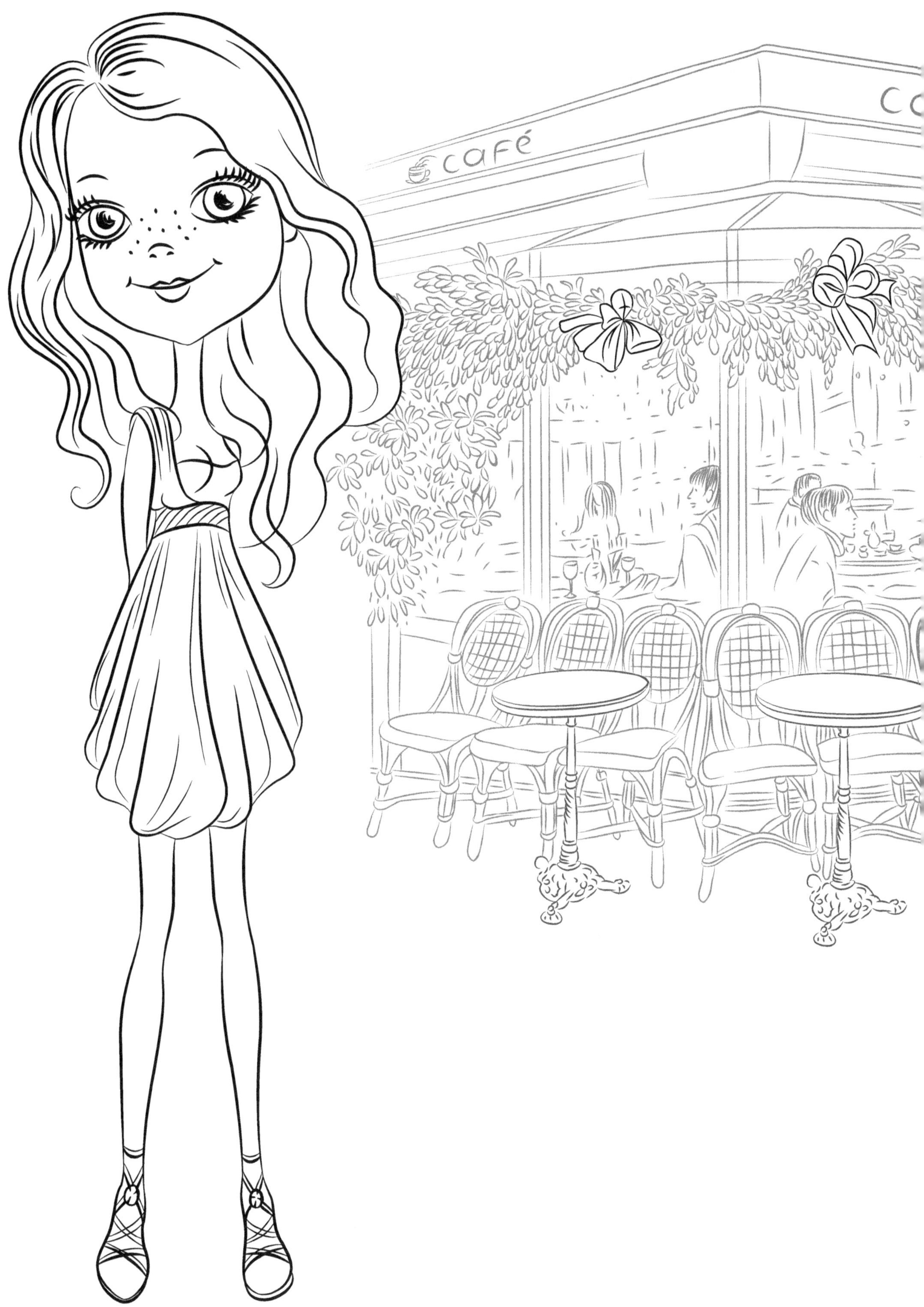
café

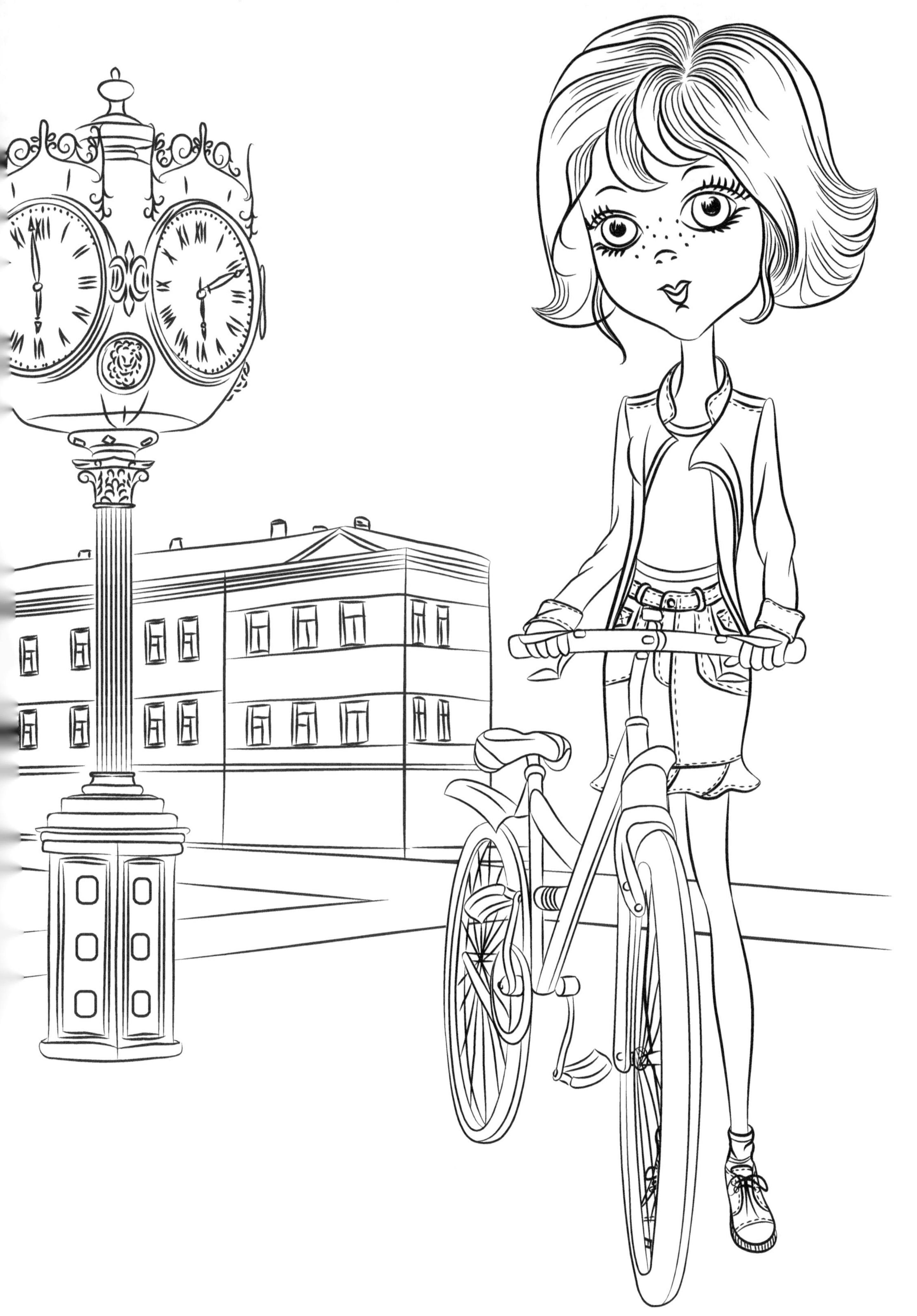

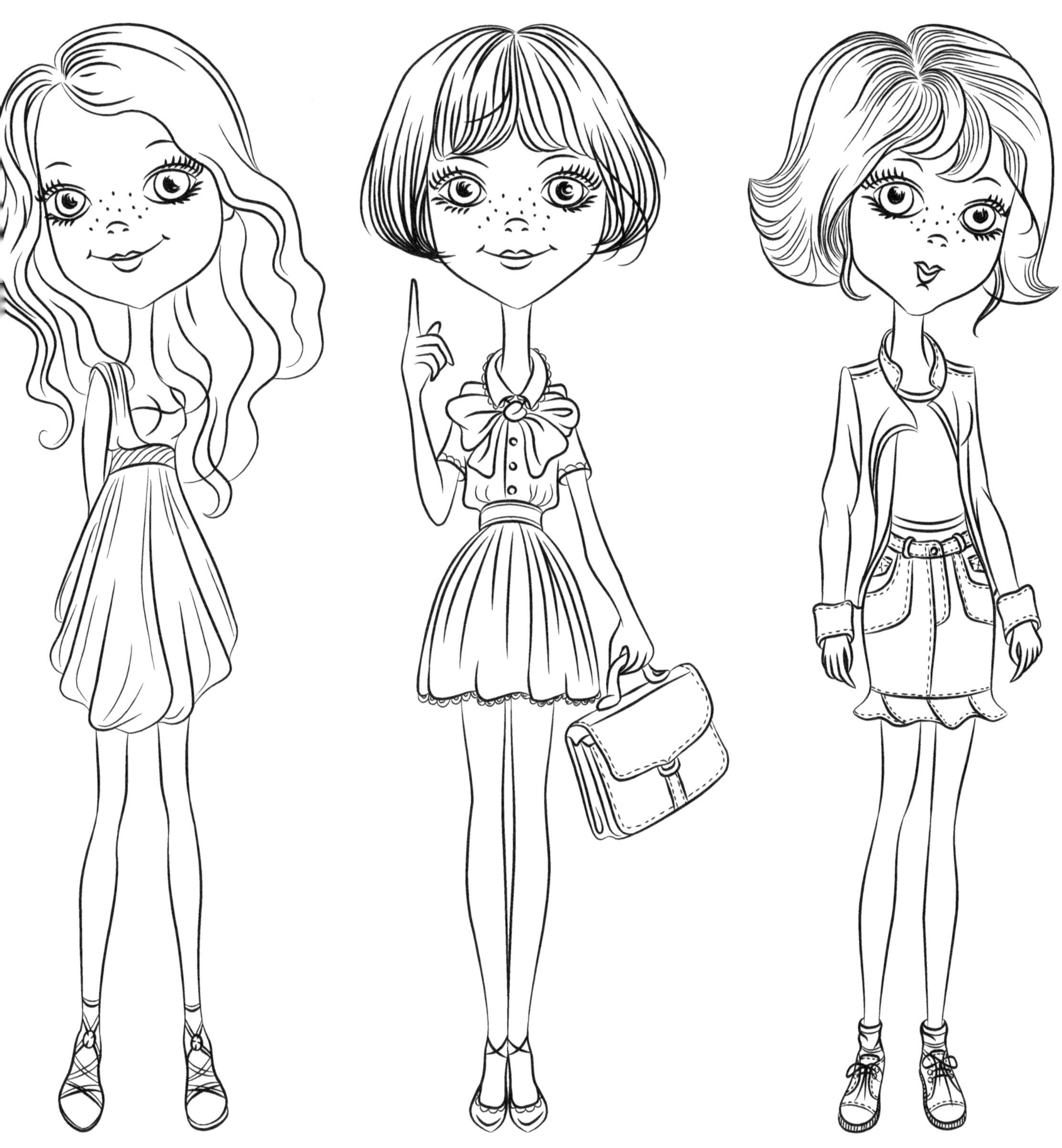

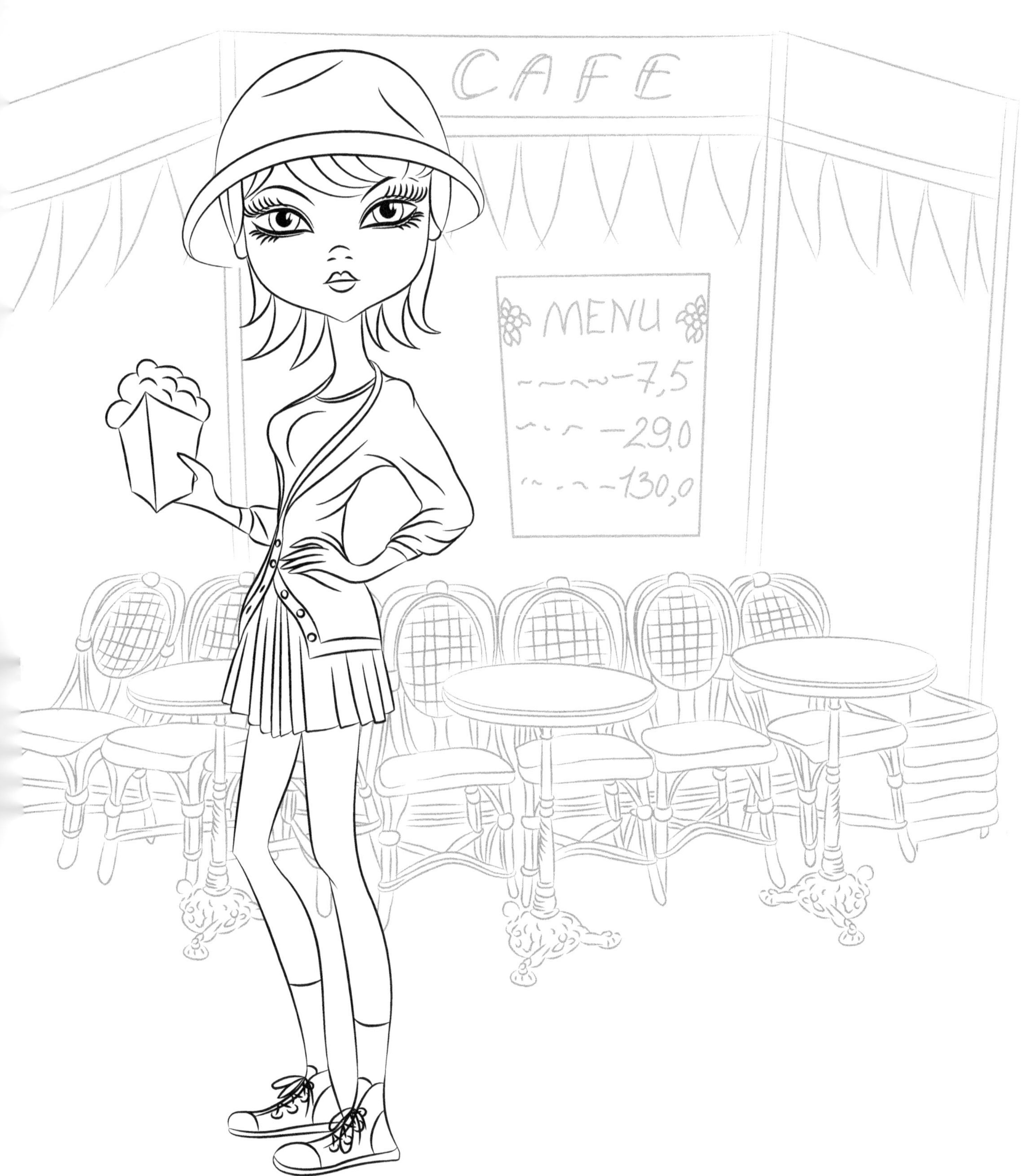
CAFE
MENU
7,5
29,0
130,0

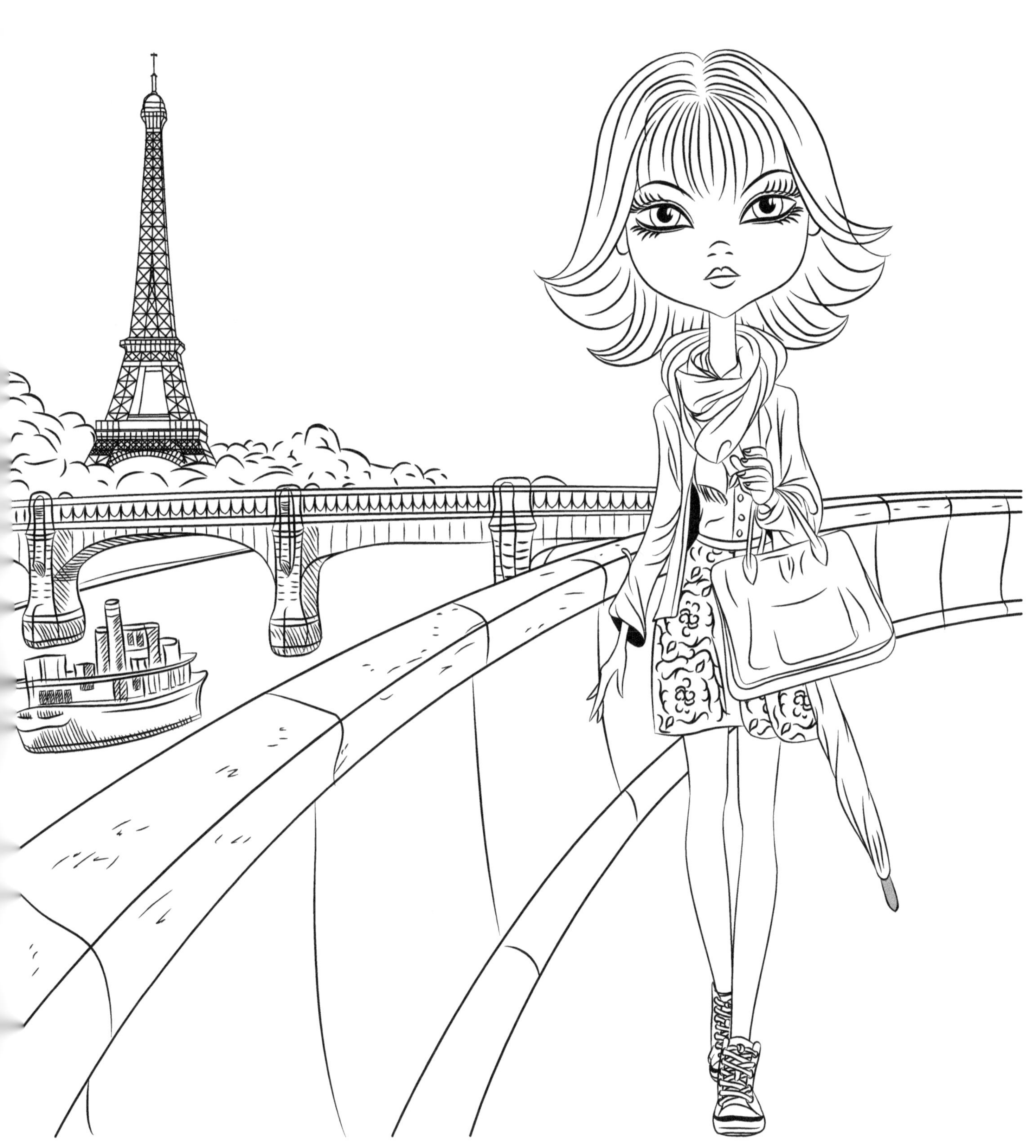

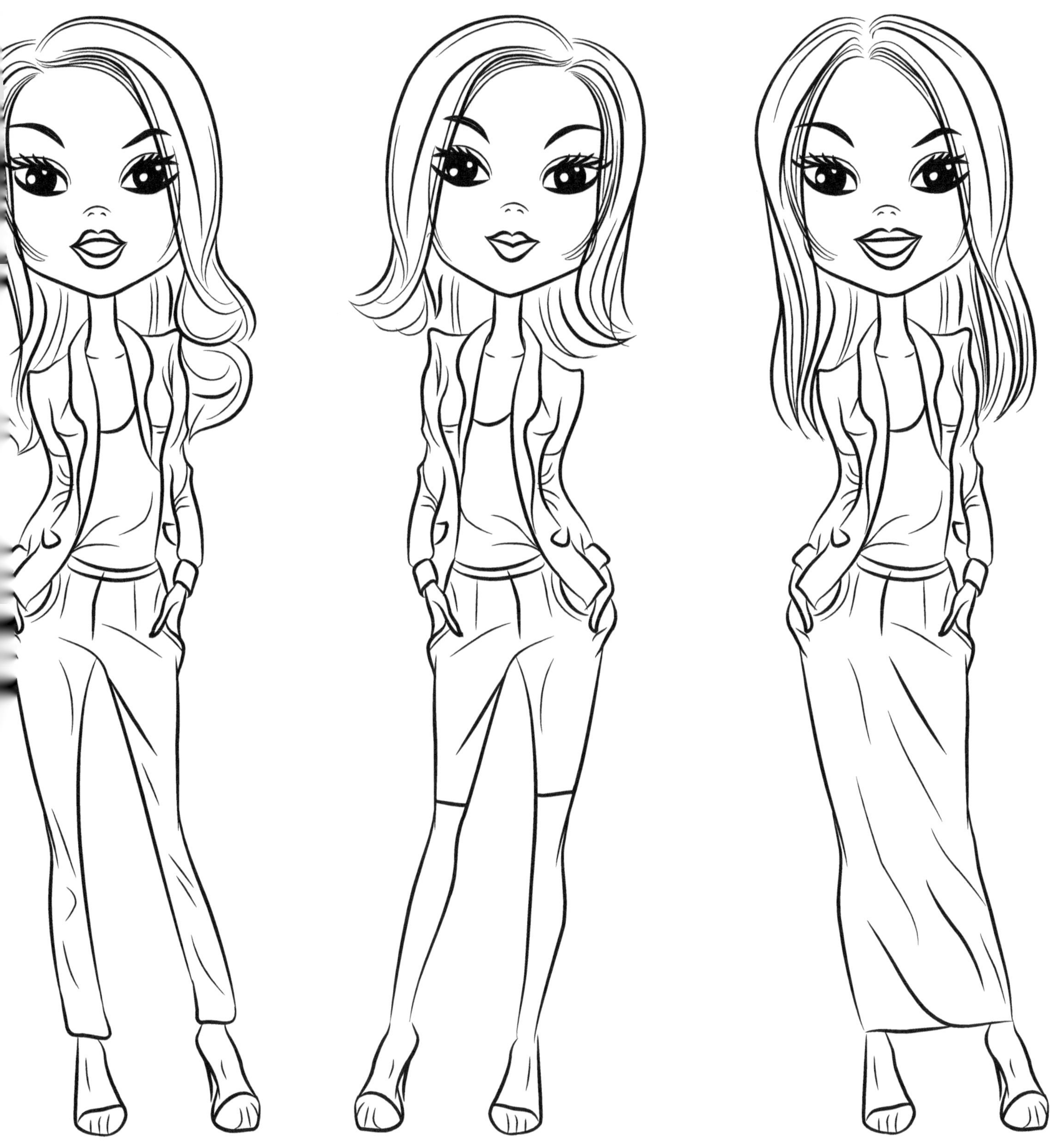

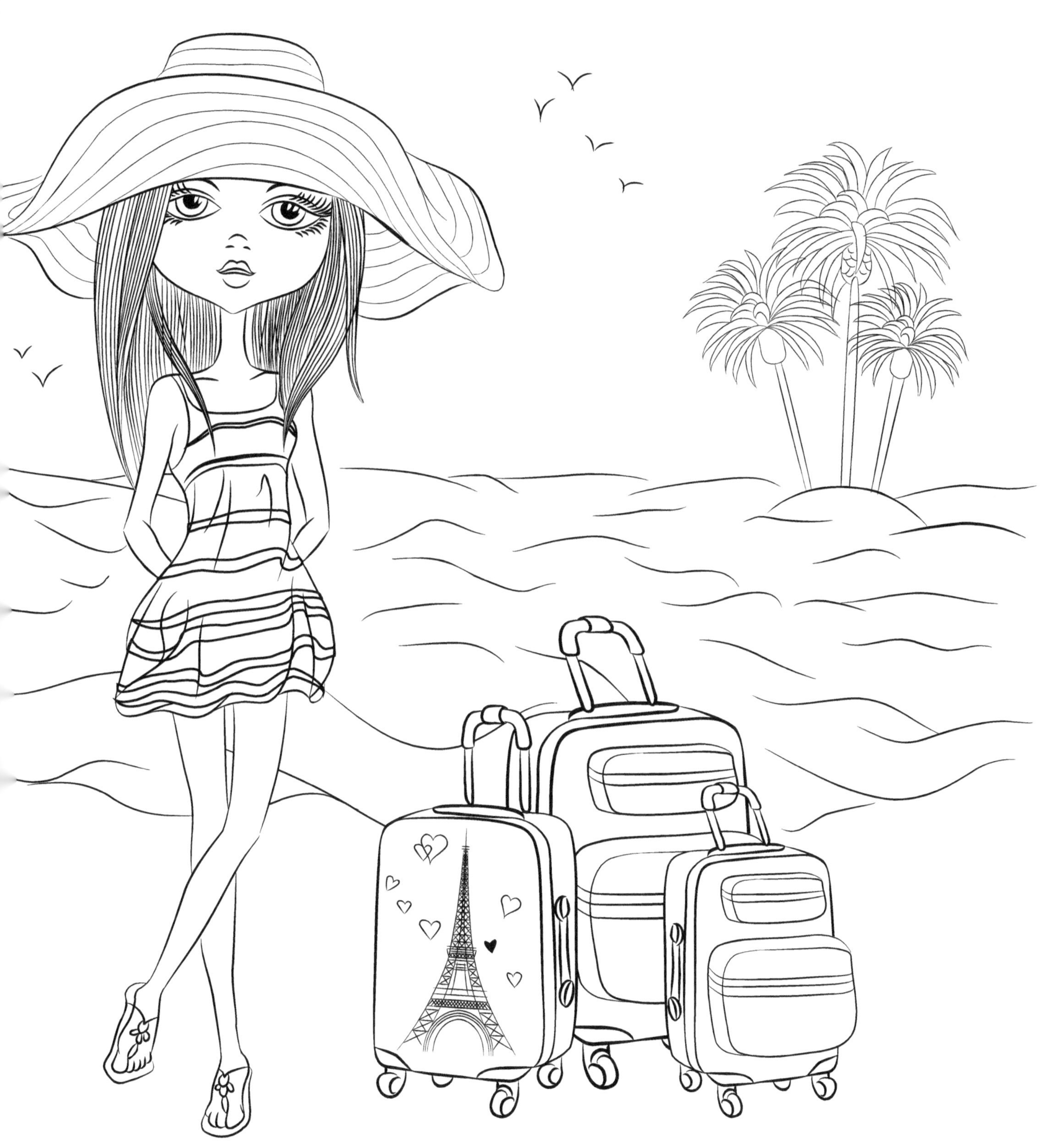

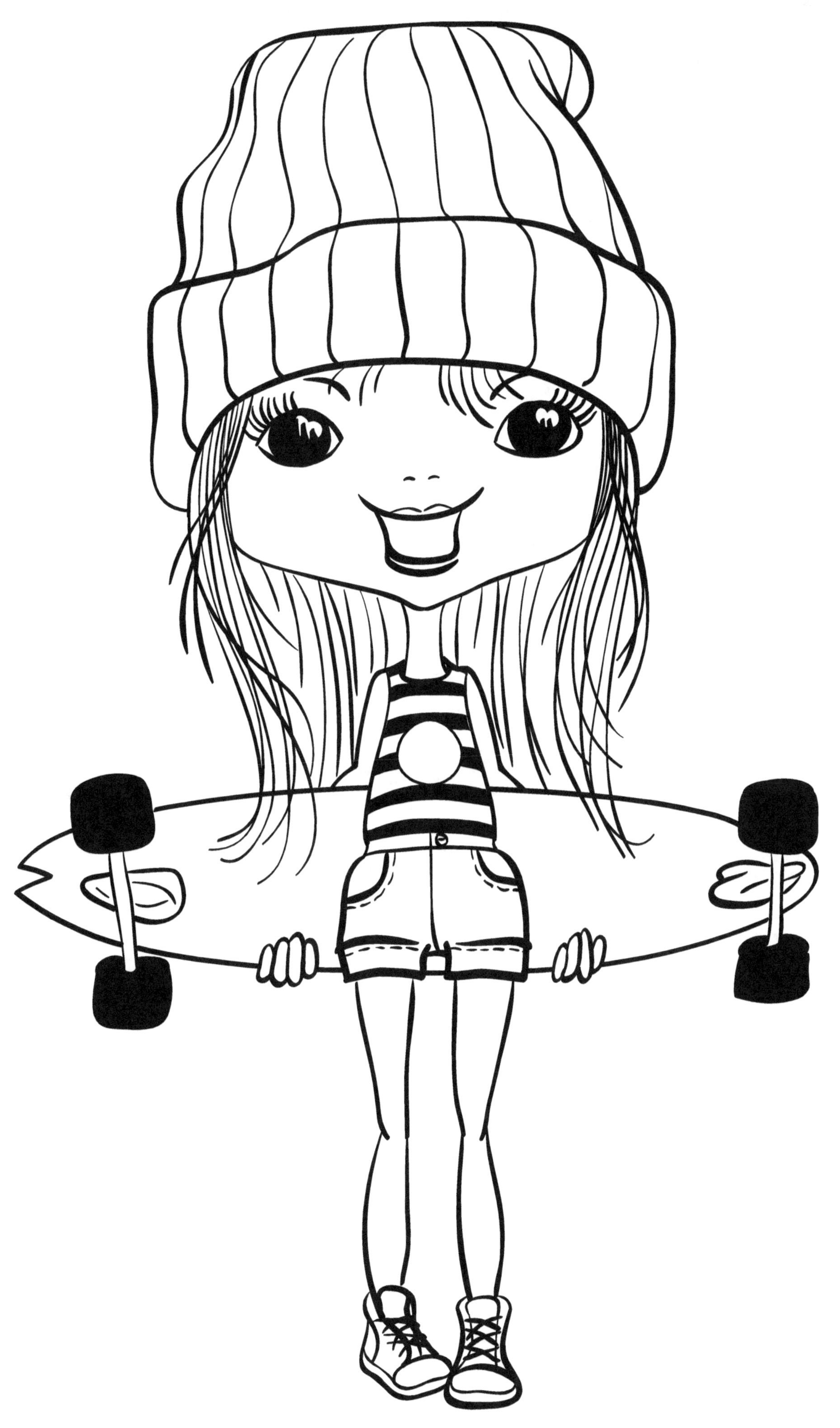

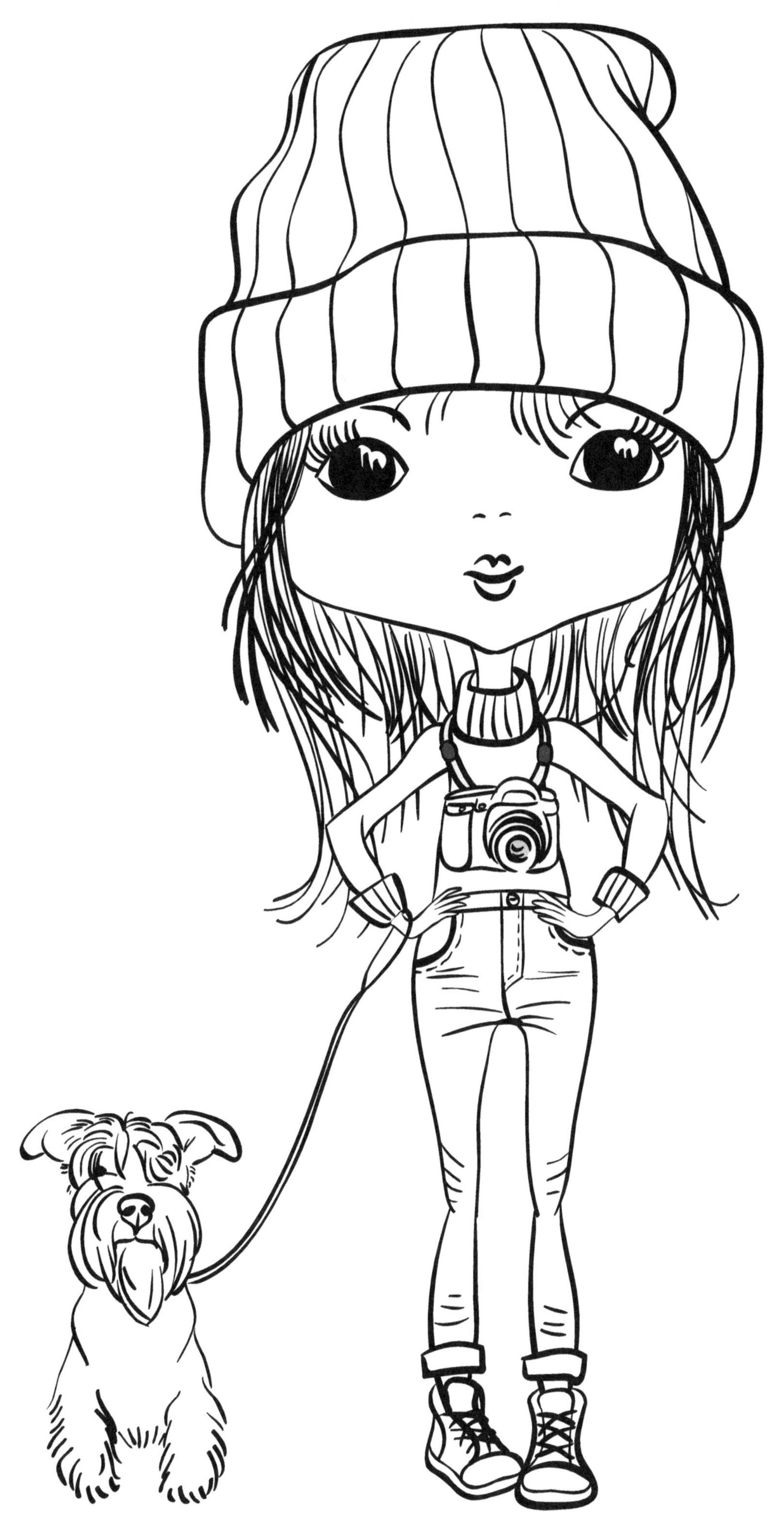

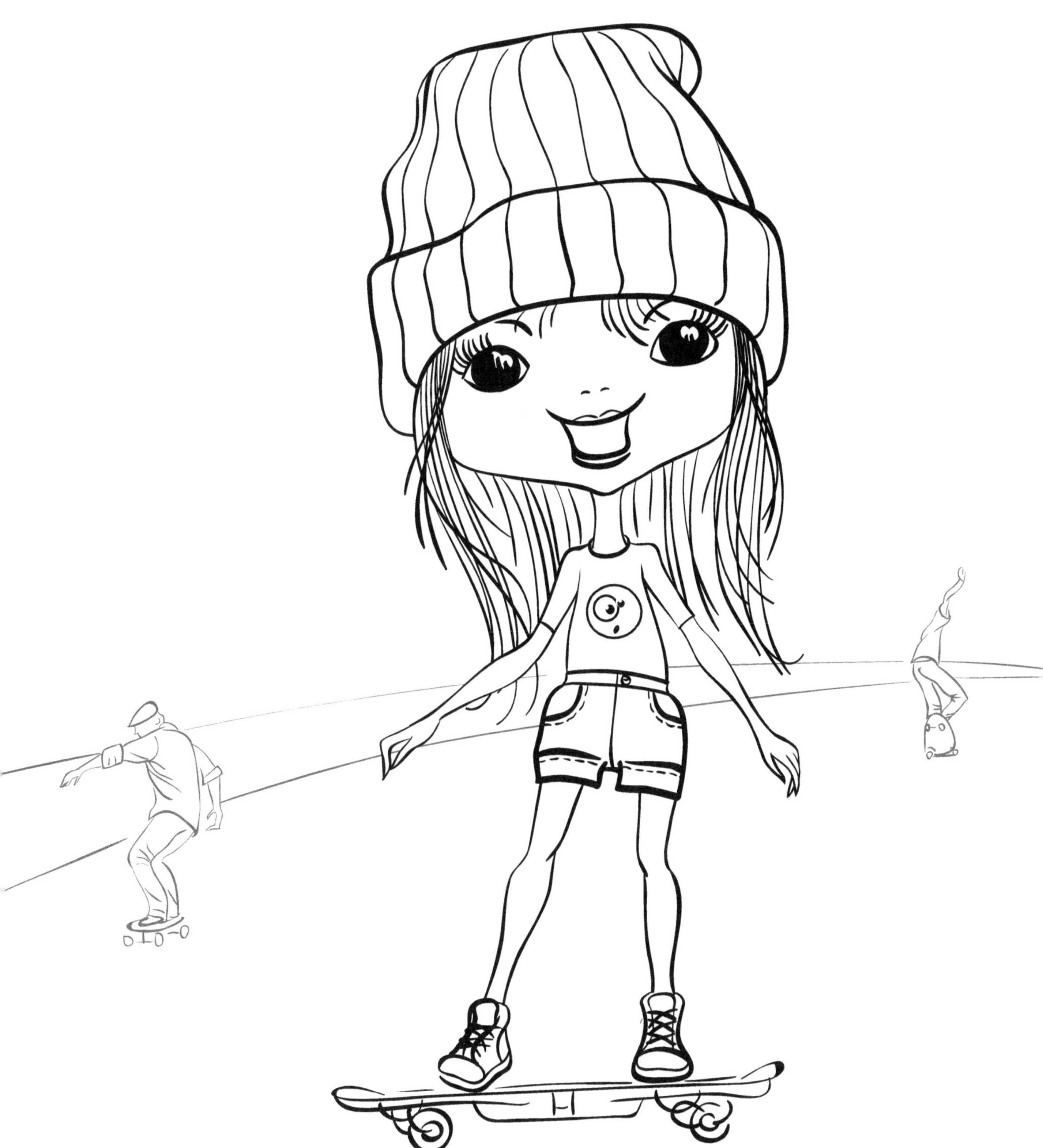

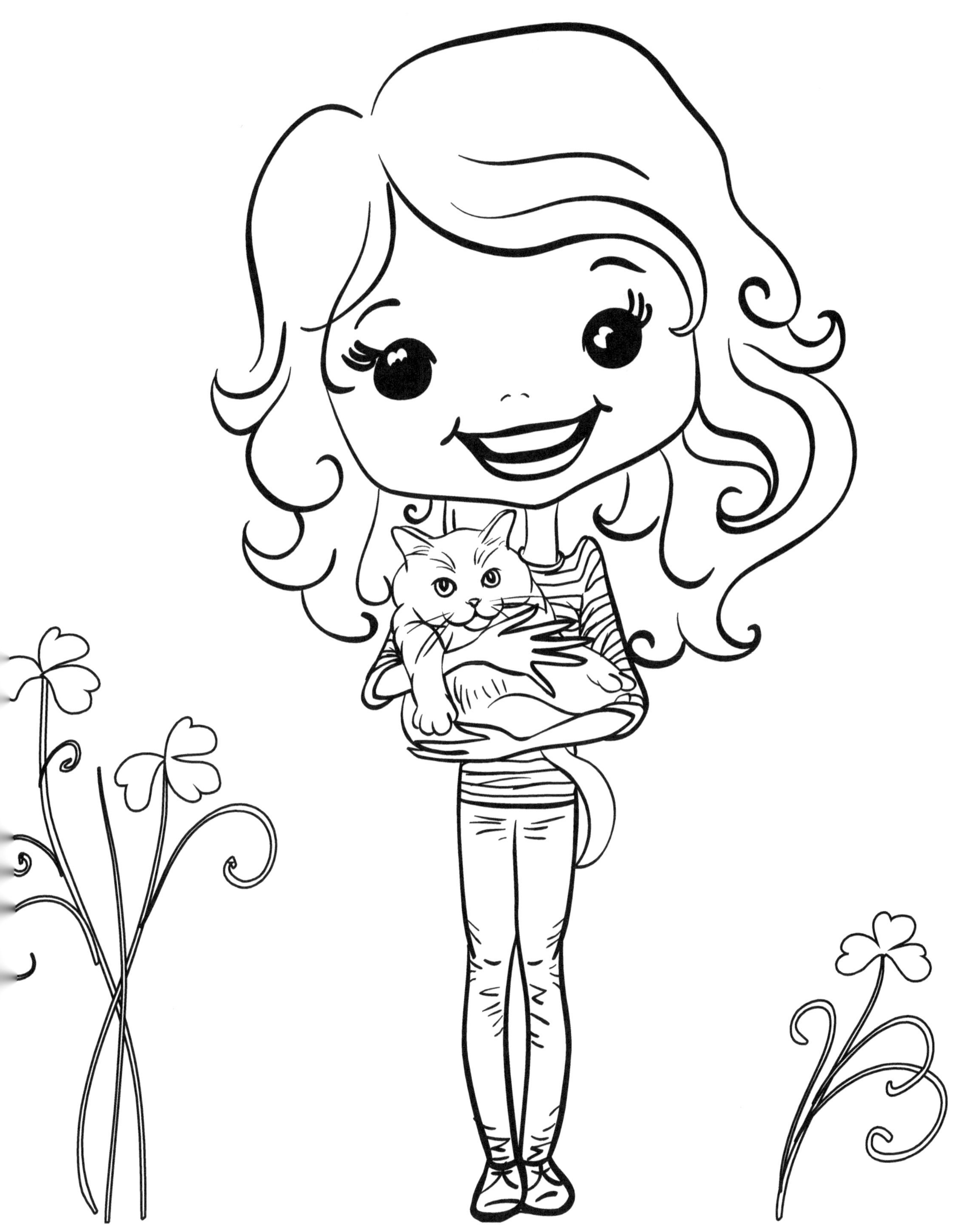

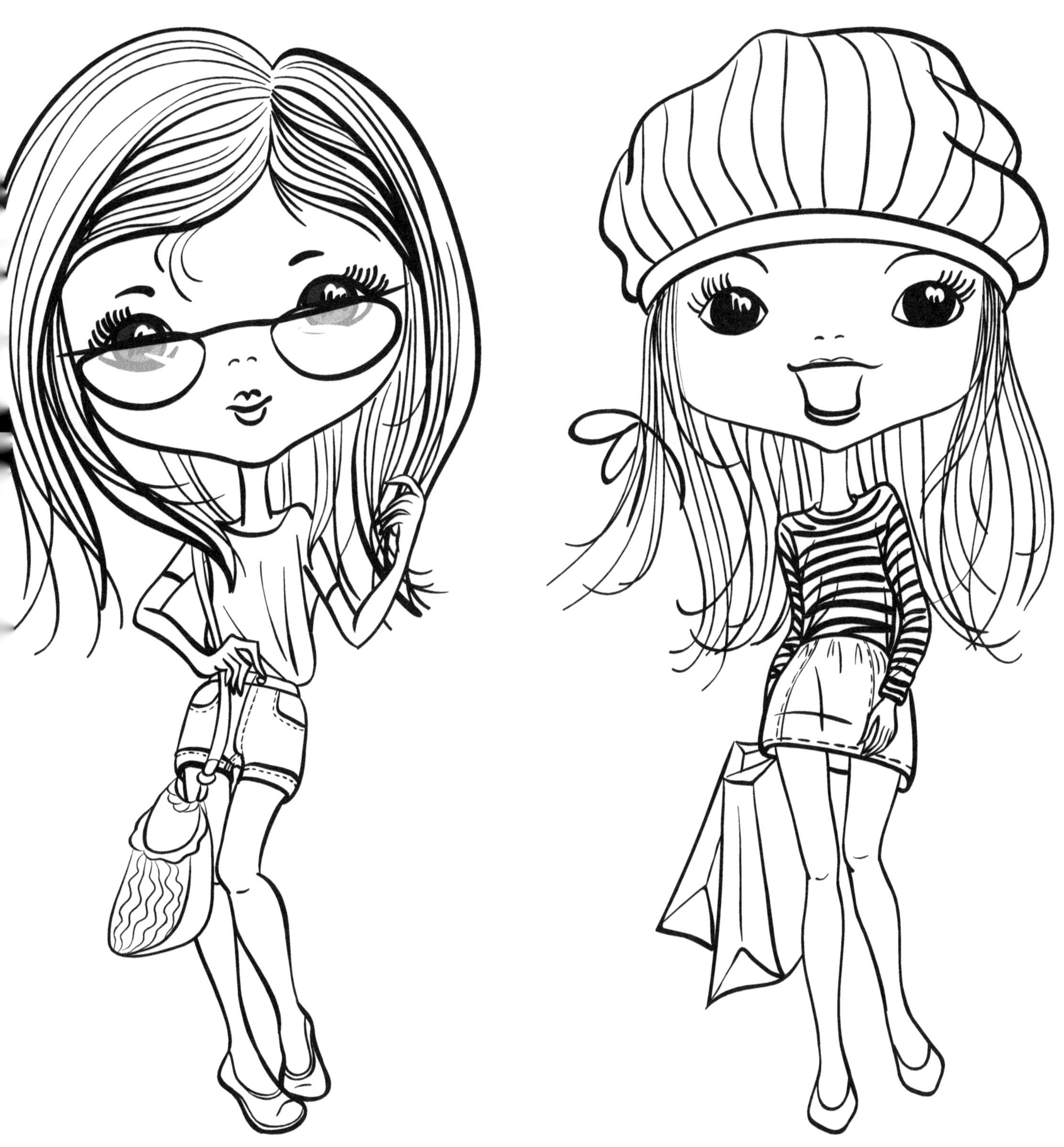

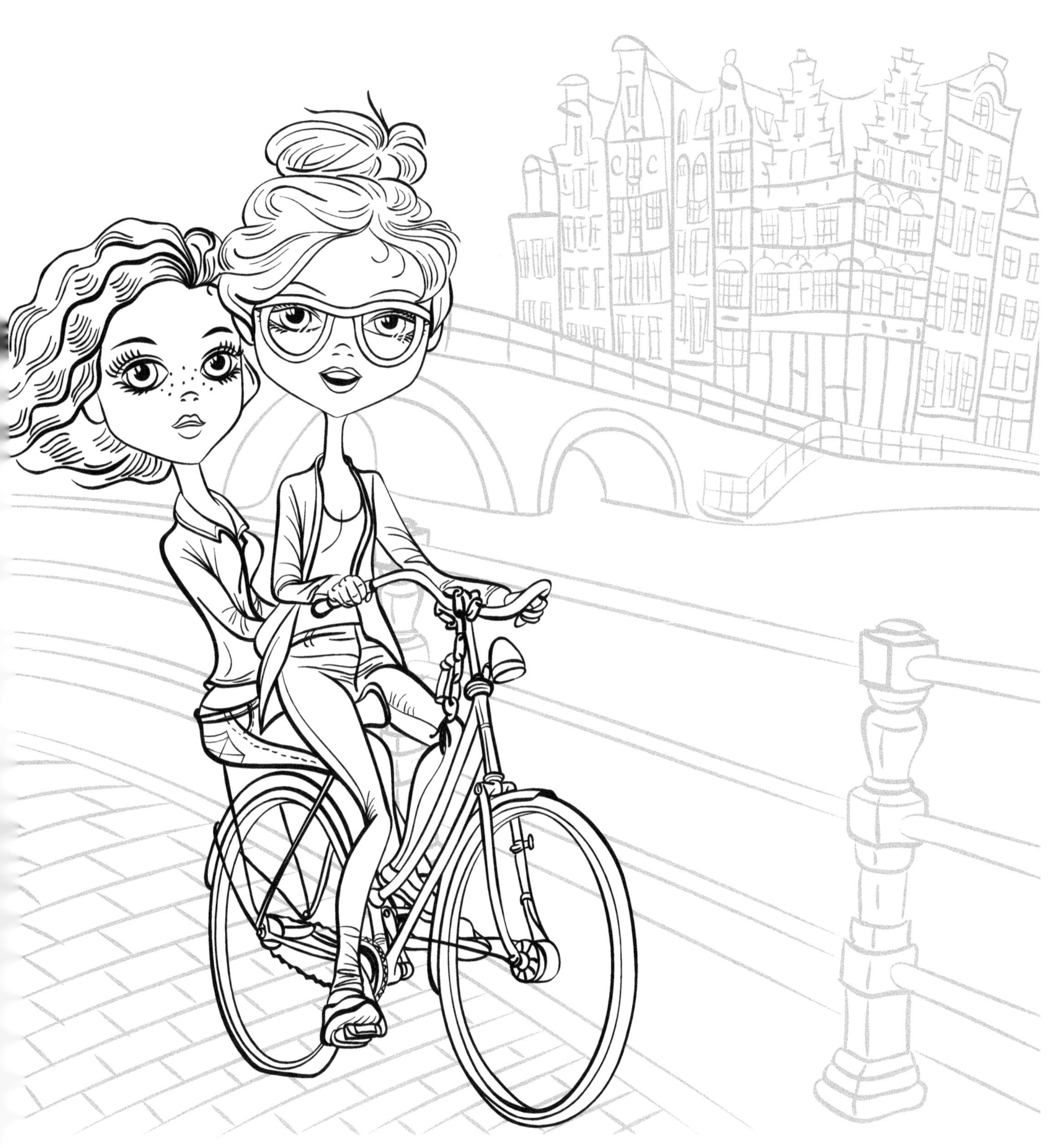

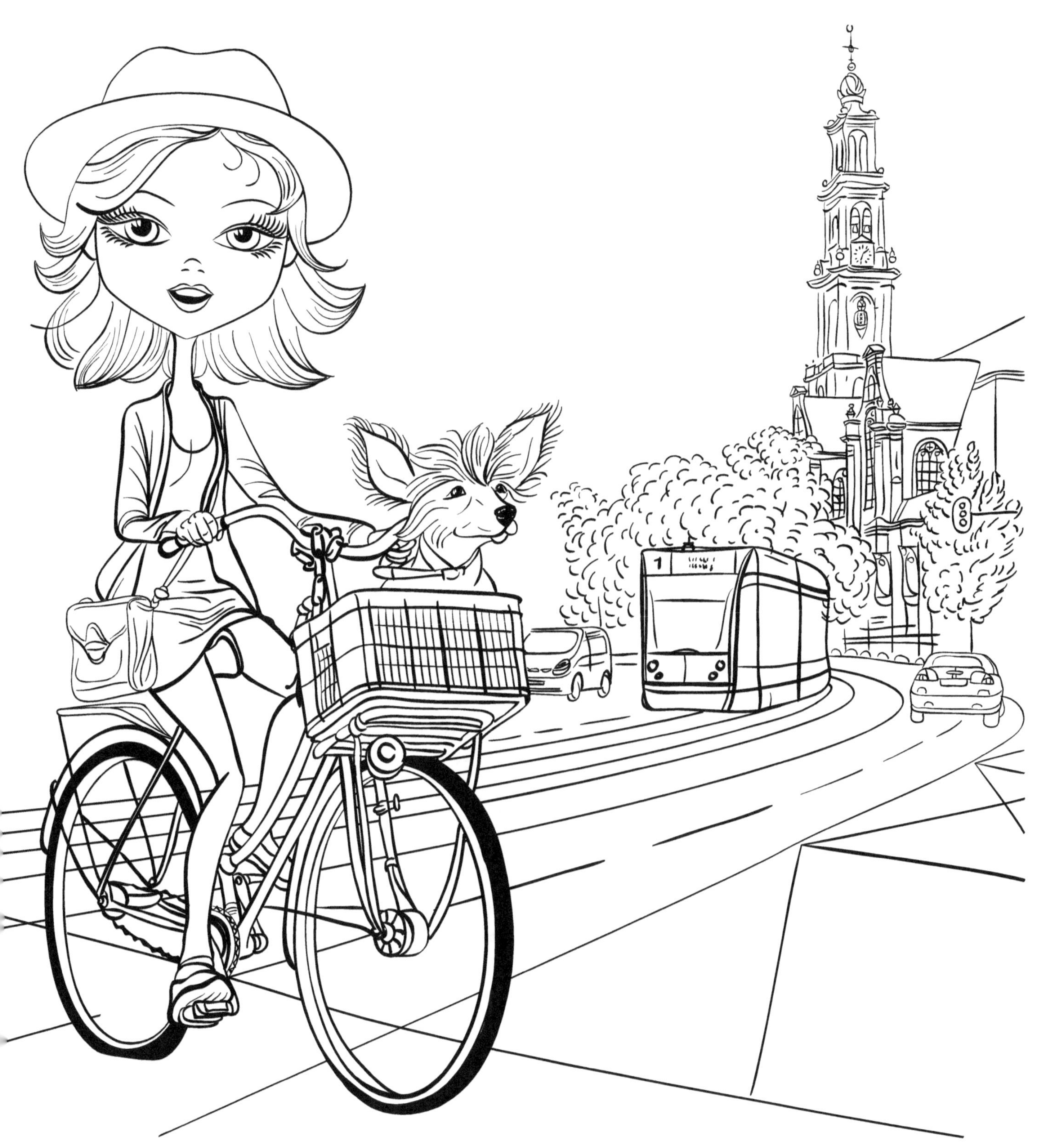

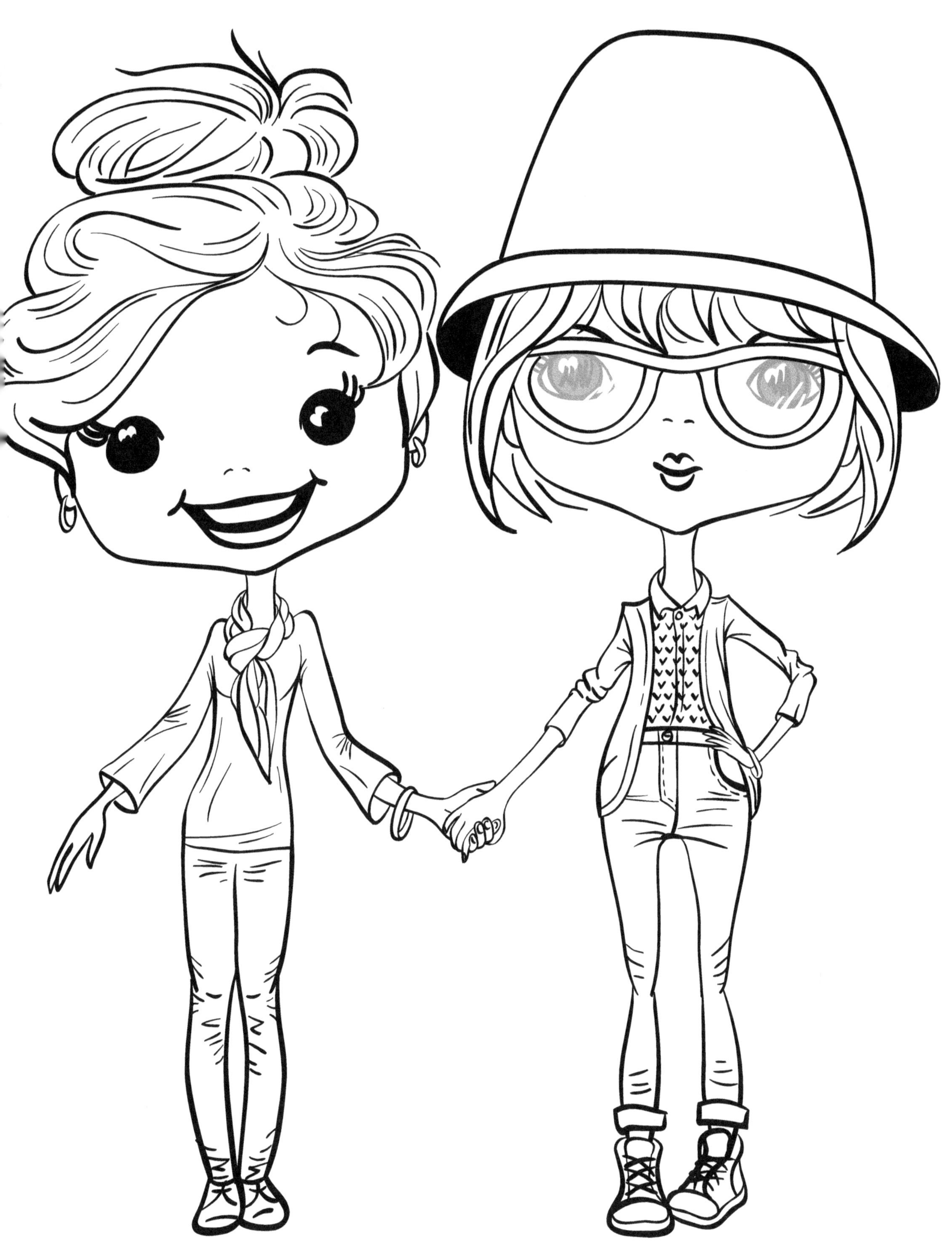

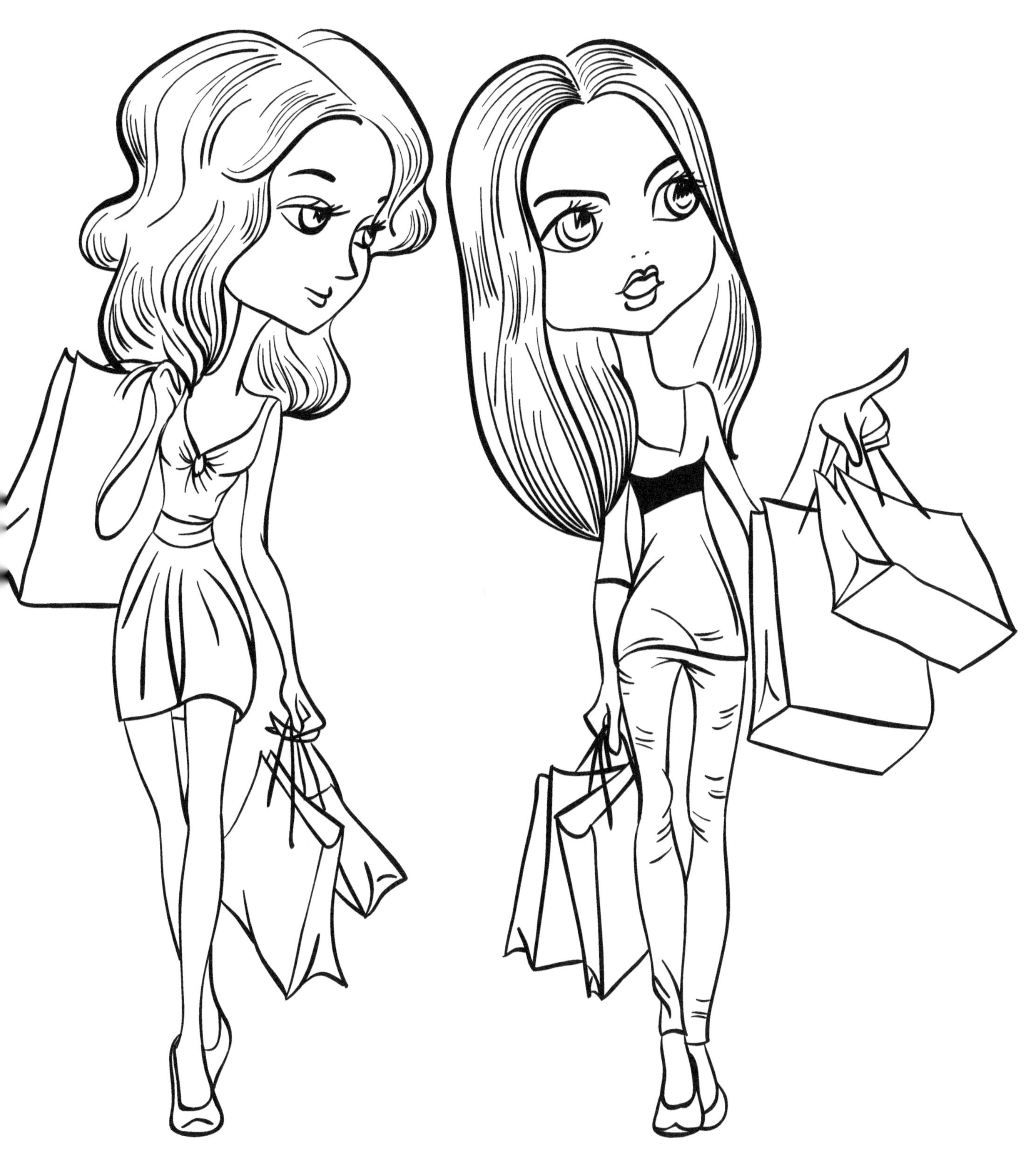

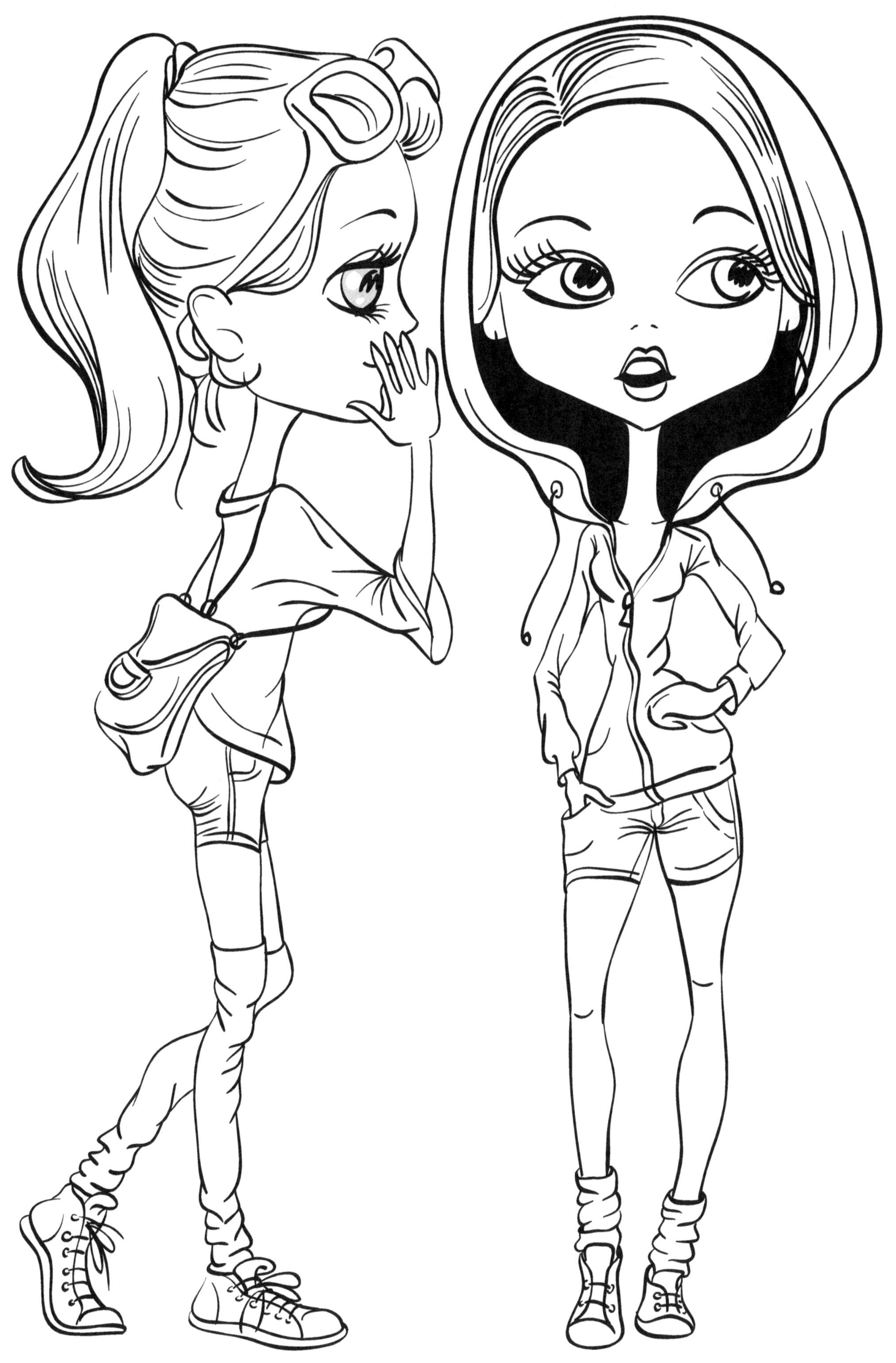

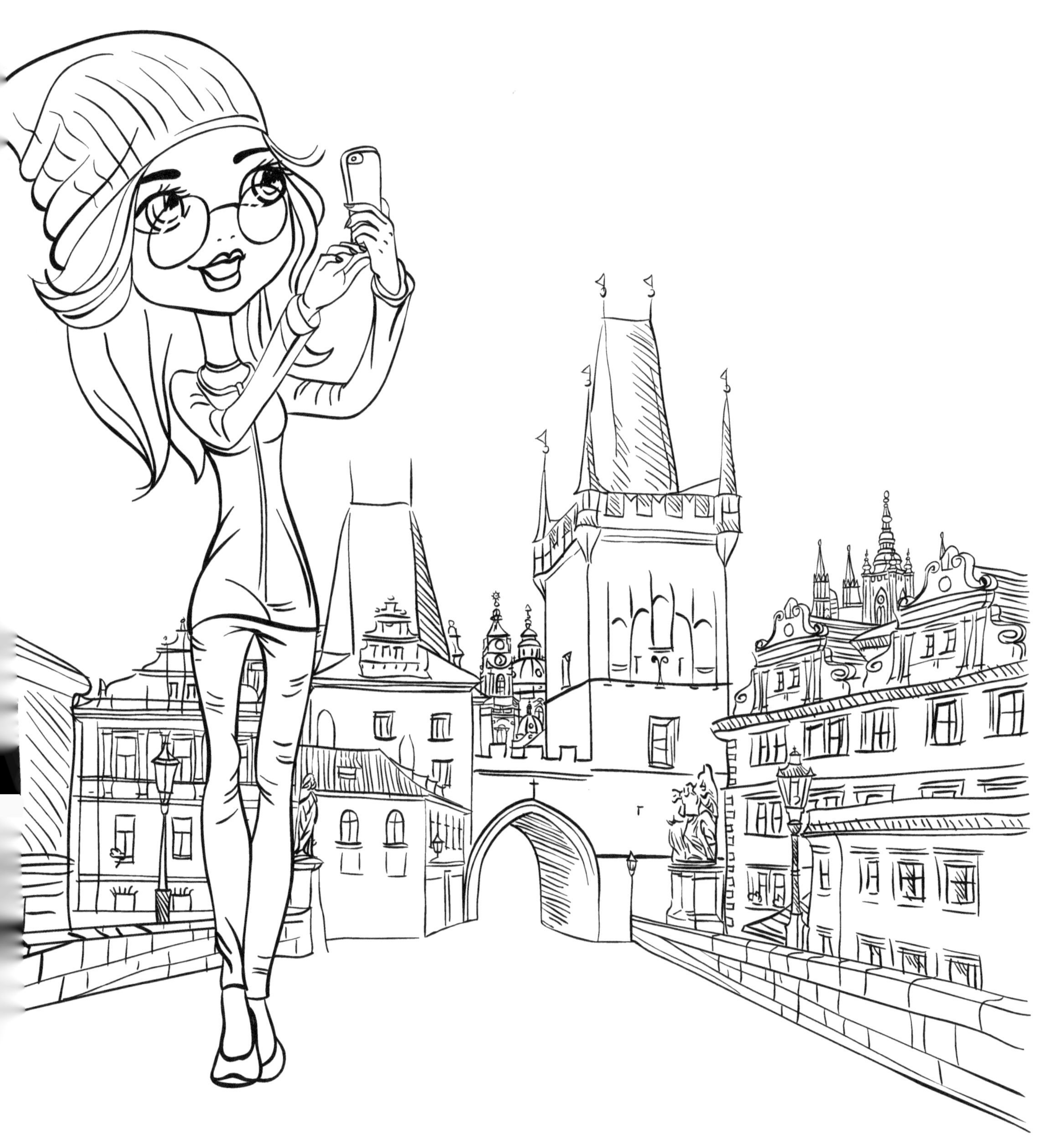

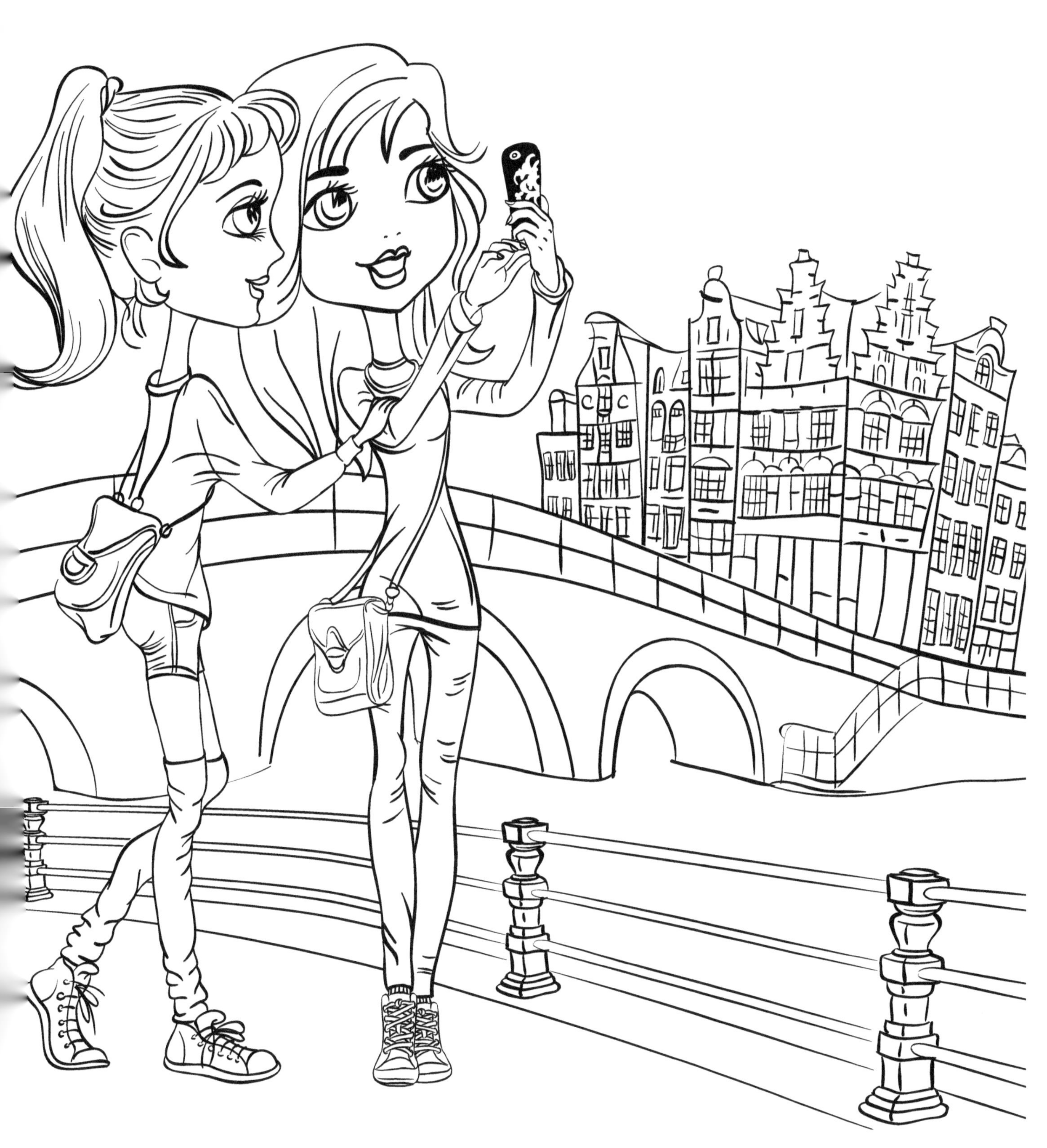

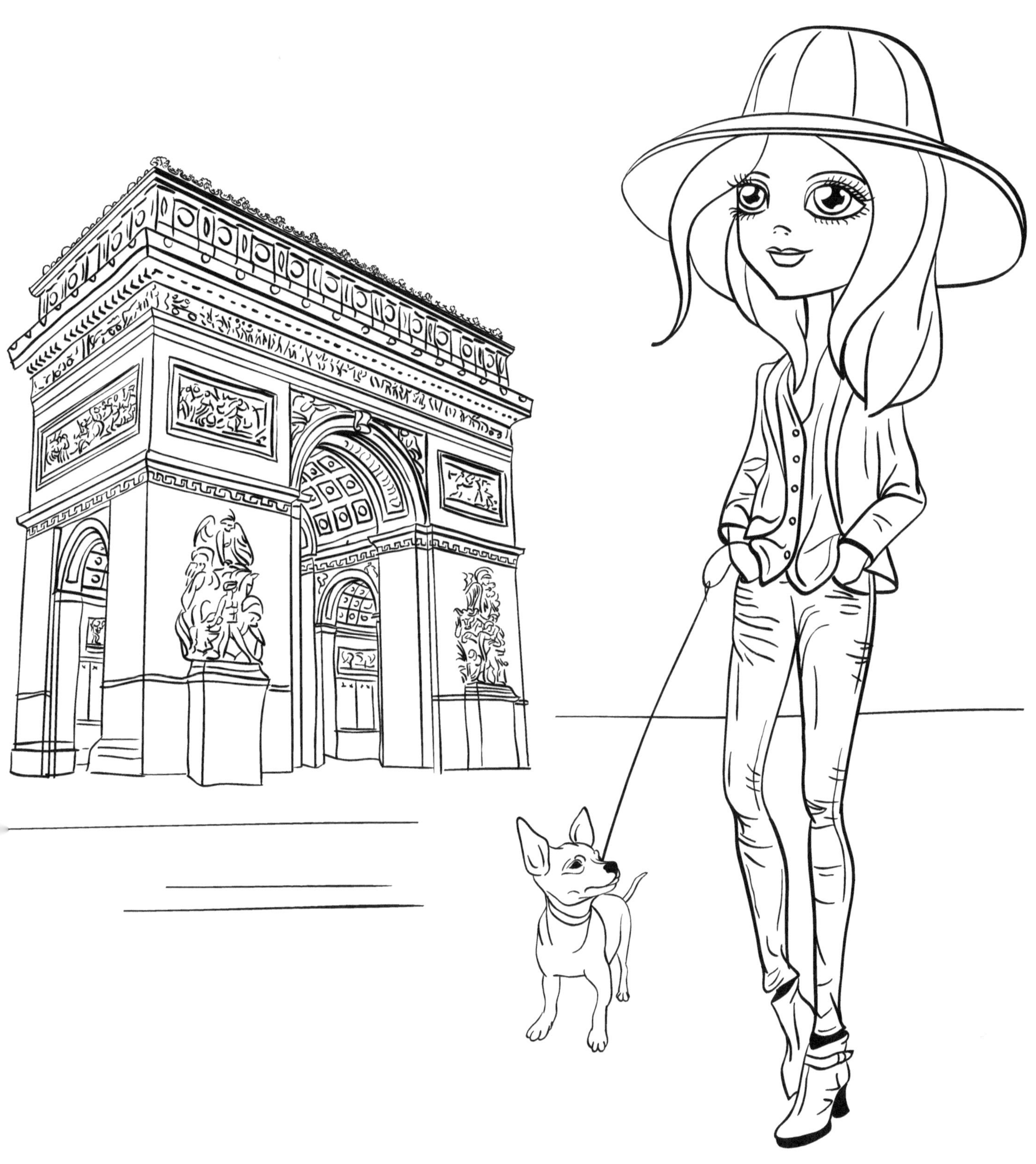

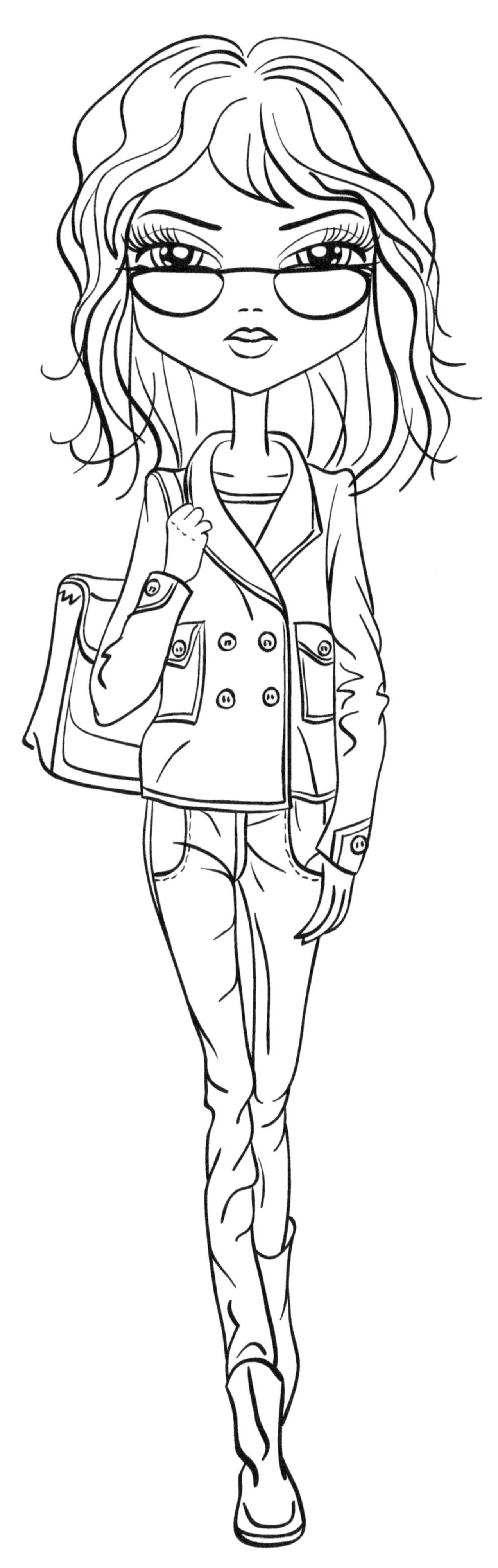

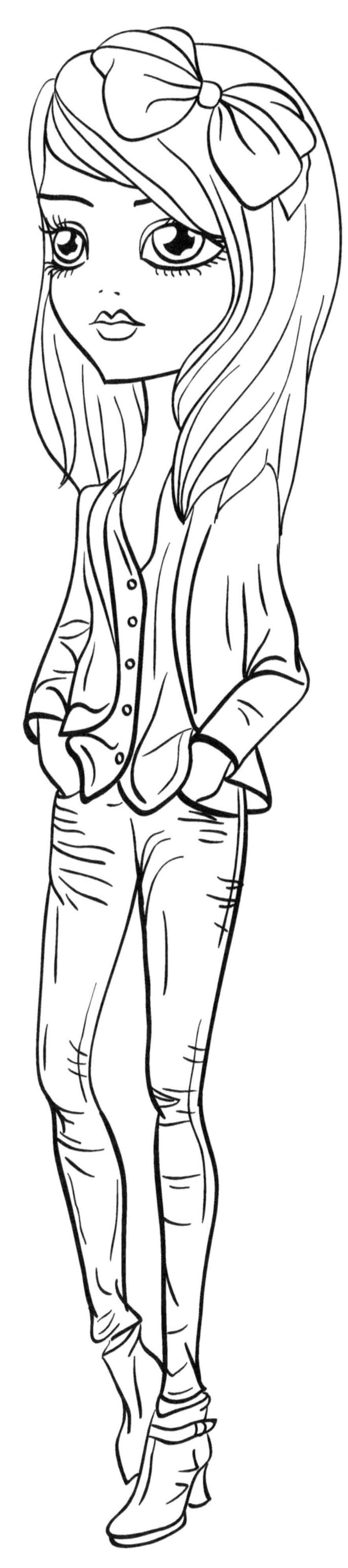

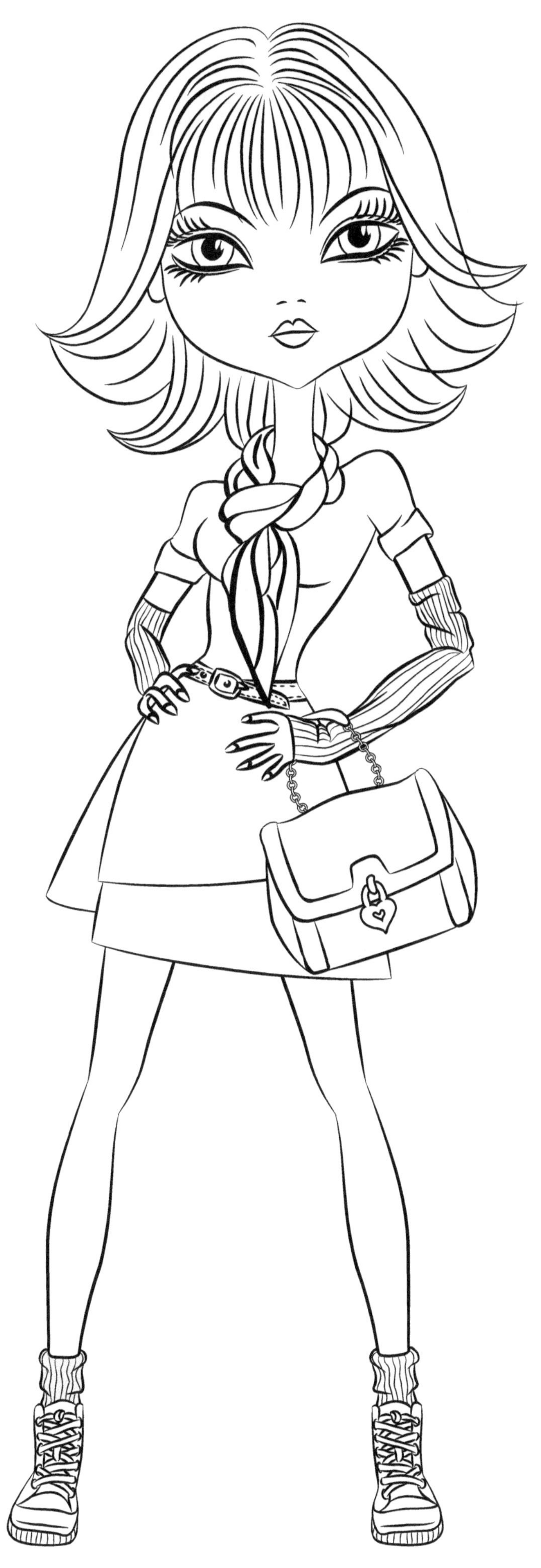

www.ingramcontent.com/pod-product-compliance
Lightning Source LLC
LaVergne TN
LVHW061255100826
845148LV00008B/1135

9781785951237